WE CHOSE CANADA

Eleven Profiles from Manitoba's Mosaic

Lesley Hughes

Aivilo Press

© 2005 Winnipeg Chinese Cultural and Community Centre

Book Design - Dennis Kashton
Printed and bound in Canada by Hignell Printers

Canadian Cataloguing in Publication Data

Hughes, Lesley, 1942-
    We chose Canada : eleven profiles from
Manitoba-
        Biography. I. Title
FC3355.H83 2005   971.27'03'0922
C2005-907214-8

ISBN 0-9686942-8-4

The Winnipeg Chinese Cultural and Community Centre wishes to acknowledge financial support for this book from Manitoba Culture, Heritage and Tourism's Heritage Grants Program, Manitoba Labour and Immigration's Ethnocultural Community Support Program, the Winnipeg Foundation, and the Thomas Sill Foundation.

Aivilo Press PO Box 897 Teulon, Manitoba R0C 3B0

Acknowledgement

This exciting project came about as a result of a chance discussion amongst a group of friends sitting around a table one day in the Winnipeg Chinese Cultural and Community Centre. Immigration issues are always a topic on which everyone seems to have an opinion. It seemed to us that with all the talented and successful people we have in Winnipeg and Manitoba that we have benefited so much from the people from overseas who have chosen to live and work and make their home here in this province.

To begin, it was decided to establish a committee. (Doesn't everyone establish an advisory committee to explore an idea?) A group was recruited who adopted the concept and went to work. I want to pay tribute to the members of that group: David Cheop LL.B, Dean Patrick Choy M.D., Olga Fuga C.M., Philip Lee C.M., The Honourable Pearl McGonigal C.M., O.M., The Honourable W. Scott Wright, and Professor William Neville. They shared their enthusiasm for the project, their knowledge of the various communities that make up our city and our province, and their feeling that immigration had been a very positive influence in this community. Moreover, they were all very committed to dispel the negative myths that often surround immigration.

Our next task was to find a qualified researcher and writer. Eventually we were fortunate to be able to obtain the services of Ms. Lesley Hughes, well known in journalistic circles in Winnipeg, to fill that position. Her role included conducting interviews with those people whose stories would be featured in the book and writing the chapters which follow.

The committee was also fortunate to be able to work with Martin Strauss, as Project Coordinator, who was a fountain of knowledge and helped us maneuver through the many channels required to reach the goal.

The project would not have been possible without our

funders: The Winnipeg Foundation, the Thomas Sill Foundation, and the Provincial Government of Manitoba. We are very grateful for their assistance, without which the Book would have been in jeopardy, or possibly not have appeared at all.

We are also indebted to the Winnipeg Chinese Cultural and Community Centre for making their rooms available for our meetings. The Chinese tea they served to us was also a very enticing drawing card, probably responsible for the well-attended meetings.

And finally, we express our thanks and complete admiration to the most important component of our project, those outstanding citizens who chose to share their personal stories of coming to Canada and the exceptional contributions they have made to our community.

It is our hope that the example of these eleven people will go a measurable distance in dispelling the myth that newcomers to Canada will take jobs away from Canadian-born citizens and endanger their livelihoods. We believe it is quite the opposite.

William Norrie C.M., O.M., Q.C., LL.D. Chair, Advisory Committee

Introduction

Human migration, often encompassing great masses of people, has been a fact of human existence throughout the millennia. Though the imperatives behind such migrations have varied greatly, historically - and pre-historically, it appears - they were often driven by the fundamental challenges of survival. In the modem era, economic, political and military factors have been particularly significant not least in the displacement of large populations from their traditional homes and in the emergence of imperialism and the development of empires. The creation of the European colonial empires in particular had profound effects on indigenous populations in Africa, Asia and the Americas. In the latter especially, colonization and subsequent political changes resulted in great waves of European immigration which overwhelmed indigenous peoples and came to dominate and shape new societies.

To these developments, the 20th Century added revolutions, world wars, civil wars, acts of genocide, the emergence of totalitarianism and, after 1945, the gradual process of decolonization in Africa and Asia. The political upheavals associated with many of these developments produced countless refugees and gave rise to the displacement or statelessness of untold millions of people. These in tum, generated new movements of large masses of people. These new migrations touched every continent and went in various directions including, in an interesting and ironic reversal of circumstance, many immigrants from Asia and Africa - including many from former European colonies - moving to and settling in Europe. Though there are, no doubt, exceptions to all rules, the accommodation of newcomers to already existing societies has rarely been simple or easy and few are the societies in which newcomers have not met with prejudice, discrimination, suspicion or open hostility.

Reminders of some of the most extreme manifestations of prejudice and suspicion are provided in recent times by the attempts of successive Canadian governments, through apology or compensation, to atone for past injustices against ethnic minorities, notably those from countries with whom Canada had been at war. In the autumn of 2005, a different kind of reminder was provided by rioting in Paris and many other French cities, in which young French citizens of North African or Middle Eastern origins, protested the reality of second class citizenship and the corresponding neglect they have long experienced at the hands of French society and government.

In many countries and at different times, one of the most frequently articulated concerns, in the hierarchy of discrimination and suspicion, has been the fear that immigrants to a new society posed threats to the jobs, opportunities and well-being of the native-born citizens of that society. This fear has fuelled significant political movements in a number of countries and, in the not-so-distant past, was a concern not unknown to Canada and to many Canadians, even though the manifold benefits of immigration and the innumerable contributions of immigrants was already a commonplace.

Yet, it was, nonetheless, out of several discussions of such phenomena that this book had its beginnings. The question to which these discussions gave rise was simple: might it not be interesting and useful to profile a number of Canadians - born elsewhere - who have, in coming to Canada, made substantial, significant and enduring impacts on Manitoba, Canada and, indeed, beyond?

The answer - or an answer, at any rate - is now before you. Here are to be found the stories of eleven women and men who came to Canada for diverse personal reasons - for freedom from persecution, or for creative opportunities and personal renewal, or for education or personal safety or for a new start and a new life. And in the pursuit and realization of their personal dreams and objectives, they have made significant contributions in a whole range of endeavours: education and research; science and medicine; culture and the arts; commerce; and public service.

This volume celebrates a small group of people who provided leadership and contributed to significant advances in their fields of activity, and whose names have achieved some measure of prominence in those fields and within the wider community. These are all people who have made a difference. If it is true that they have been enriched by the experience of becoming Canadians, it is no less true that Canada has been enriched by their labours, talent and devotion to the country we share. Moreover, this small group, though they have achieved prominence, are but the tip of the proverbial iceberg: the commitment and contributions to Canadian society of untold numbers of immigrants from all over the world are truly beyond measuring but, as here, worth celebrating.

William Neville

William Neville is Associate Professor and former Head of the Department of Political Studies at the University of Manitoba

Preface

Once upon a time, not that long ago, somebody in Winnipeg had a wonderful idea, which was, essentially to listen to the stories of eleven very successful immigrants to Manitoba.

There was a wish to document their achievements and to honour them. There was a wish to encourage others to think again about the usefulness of immigration.

And there was, of course, good old fashioned human curiosity to know these stories and see what might be learned from them. The stories are published here, and every reader will have a personal view of exactly what lessons they have produced.

As the writer of those stories, let me give you a hint.

Four of the eleven personalities in this book were refugees; seven came for other reasons, personal and professional opportunity for growth being high on the list.

Seven of the eleven became innovators in very different fields; medicine, cross-cultural education, northern outreach, retailing, housing, and anthropology.

Every one of them has made a significant difference to the quality of life in this prairie city we call home.

Without them, we would have a much smaller reputation as a medical research centre; we would not enjoy the access to the mystery and excitement of other cultures that we enjoy now; we would not be home to one of the country's most progressive wellness centres, nor to a sculpture garden that is matchless in the world. You will probably recognize and add other gifts they brought with them.

Lengthy interviews with these eleven have left a profound impression on me.

They have reminded me how little we know about each other, especially people in public life.

I was surprised to learn that one of our most devout and

popular Muslim leaders had a Catholic education. I was surprised and ashamed to learn that it was once illegal for Japanese Canadians to own property in the city of Winnipeg. It surprised me also that one of the city's most productive and benevolent citizens had been a conscript in Hitler's army.

I was graphically reminded of the deep suffering people can endure and overcome.

The eleven and their stories have reminded me of the many features of Canadian life I take for granted: a variety of freedoms, safety, opportunity, social mobility, tolerance and a genuine, daily brand of multiculturalism that is unique among nations.

The stories also show us how fragile these achievements are, that even Canada can bungle them, and that if we claim to love our country, "We stand on guard for thee" must be a reality rather than a cliché.

To the eleven, without exception, thank you for coming to Canada. And thank you for opening your hearts and sharing your history so we may see our country through fresh eyes.

Lesley Hughes

Table of Contents

Yoshimaru Abe

. . . .

In the midst of the plain
Sings the skylark
Free of all things.

Basho (1644-1694)

Yoshimaru Abe is 91 now.

His straight back and his radiant face both belie his age; the cane he uses to get around the house comes as a surprise.

He leans forward when someone speaks to him. It's an effort to hear what people are saying, unless it's his diminutive wife Yoshi speaking. But then, after 64 years of marriage, her voice must seem very like his own.

Abe-san is as spare and elegant as the Haiku poetry he has

been writing for more than fifty years.

The son of a traditional Shinto family, he tends to the Buddhist shrine in his North Kildonan home every morning after taking his tea.

Abe-san was born in a small village on the southern island of Japan, and left it to join his adventurous and travel loving father in Canada in the spring of 1927. When he arrived at his parents' farm in Port Hammond, British Columbia, he was beside himself with excitement. He had the eye of a poet and an artist even then, and the lush beauty of his new home touched him to the core.

He was 13 years old when he arrived in Canada. He had no idea just how unwelcome he would be.

Yoshimaru Abe would be innocent of any disloyalty, but the country he had chosen to call home would make him a prisoner of guilt and force him to build his own cell.

He was not a refugee when he came to Canada, but Canada would withhold his citizenship and make him one.

Events that had nothing to do with him, some of them thousands of miles away in other countries would define and limit his life.

Rather, they would try.

In truth, his little known story is a most unusual one. In it, humility triumphs over humiliation, creativity springs from oppression, and patience transforms injustice.

In the right hands, it seems, life can really happen that way.

* * * * * * * * *

From the early 1900s a few Japanese families had settled in the rich Fraser Valley to farm and their number increased steadily until, around 1940, there were almost five hundred of them. Many were talented gardeners and they worked hard. The result was a considerable agricultural prosperity and an apparently bright future. Among other things, they established the Maple Ridge Berry Growers Co-operative, a step which they believed would secure the markets for their products, products which, over sixty years ago, were bringing in more than a million dollars a year.

Yoshimaru was the youngest of four children in his family; there were two sisters and a brother.

His humiliation in Canada began the first day he went to school.

The school master put both the tall thirteen year old and his brother in grade one.

His brother felt shamed and soon dropped out, but Yoshimura stayed put. He caught up quickly, continued in public school for four years and, when he was finished with school, found a good job in a local sawmill, at the same time continuing to help out with the family farm.

Though the rumbles of war could be heard from Europe and Japan, life was normal and life was good in the Fraser Valley. In October of 1941, Abe-san's foreman at the saw mill, Mr. Ito, served as a *biashakunin*, a go-between to arrange a marriage between the young man and Yoshi Homma, the lovely first daughter of a much respected Japanese Canadian family.

Yoshi's father, Tomekichi Homma was a well known leader in BC's Japanese community. His father in law would prove to be an important influence in Abesan's life.

The couple were married in January of 1942, but their happiness was clouded. Canada had earlier joined the war against Hitler's armies; the country was at war with Japan and there were disturbing rumours that the Japanese community might present a security risk to the war effort.

People were saying Japanese nationals of military age could be sent away to work on road camps in the Rocky Mountains.

The prospect of separation left the newly weds anxious and uneasy.

One day about a month after their marriage Abesan's

boss at the sawmill approached him and told him that, if the younger nationals like himself volunteered to go to the road camps, there was a good chance that the women, children and elders would not have to go at all.

Yoshimaru wrote this account of it:

"My brother and I and a few others talked it over and we decided to go. In February, the group of about ten of us from Port Hammond reported

for the task.

"There were exactly a hundred volunteers, some from Vancouver Island and the lower Fraser Valley. We were taken to the RCMP barracks for registration and examination, and later in the afternoon we boarded the waiting train at the CN Station.

Our destination was unknown."

The volunteers soon understood they had been duped. What they had believed – that their actions might spare some members of the community was really meant to get the process of displacement off to a smooth and efficient start. They were also troubled to learn that many in their own community were deeply angry with them for appearing to co-operate with it.

"We all stayed in bunk cars on the railway sidings. The average temperature was about twenty degrees below, and the snow banks were two feet deep. Our work was to cut timbers to build our own camp. It was a few days later before the necessary materials arrived and the construction actually started. It took about a month to complete the camp.

"Finally, in early April, we left our bunk car and moved into the camp and the actual road work began.

"Eventually, trainloads of Japanese nationals were arriving daily from the coastal area and camps were built for them along the CN mainline from Jasper to Blue River near Kamloops."

In June of that year, Abe-san's wife and her parents also had to leave their home and moved into Hastings Park in

Vancouver, where the British Columbia Security Commission had set up administrative headquarters.

"They were housed in a large livestock building where conditions were deplorable. They had to stay there until the relocation camps were ready for them in the Interior."

Conditions were indeed deplorable. The Hommas were living in a stinking barn. Each family occupied a unsanitary stall that formerly sheltered a horse. Blankets were hung between the stalls in a frail attempt at privacy

"It was sometime in July when my brother and I were transferred from road camp to Tashme, about 15 miles southeast of Hope, B.C.

"Tashme was a completely isolated camp which accommodated about 3000 people at its peak. We all lived in temporary housing there until the end of the war. We stayed there for almost four years.

"The total evacuation of Japanese Canadians was complete by October of 1942. Our homes, our cars and trucks, our possessions were all taken away from us without our consent and were never returned."

Many families went into the internment camps prosperous, and came out poor. Unlike the US, Canada required their Japanese prisoners to pay for their own incarceration expenses, an act that was contrary to the principles of the Geneva Convention.

The events of Pearl Harbour had been a watershed. The day after the Japanese Air Force attacked an American military base in Hawaii, 1300 Japanese Canadians lost possession of their boats along with the hope of a future livelihood. Some boats were auctioned off or dry docked. The Canadian Navy took the best ones.

The financial losses were devastating, but they were not the hardest thing to endure.

It had been painful for Abe-san and Yoshi to be separated as newly weds, but they had eventually been re-united when the married people in the road camps were allowed to join their families in the interior.

Illness in the family exaggerated the effects of the forced separation.

While still in the Tashme camp, the couple and their two small children received a telegram saying Yoshi's father was critically ill in Slocan. He had been bedridden for some time, the result of a stroke years before the evacuation. Yoshi and Abesan went immediately to the RCMP office, taking the telegram with them.

They asked for permission for quick travel to Slocan. They were entitled to go on compassionate grounds, but for reasons that were not explained to them, the permission was not forthcoming.

A second telegram came later that night. The urgency was different now. Yoshi's beloved father had died. This time they were allowed to go.

In spite of their grief, the family rejoiced to see each other. It was at her husband's funeral that Yoshi's widowed mother saw her grandchildren for the first time,

There were countless stories of similar separation, torment and grief in the Japanese internment camps.

What made them all much worse was that, contrary to the position taken by the federal government of Canada, none of the suffering was necessary.

Neither Japanese nationals nor Japanese Canadians posed a security to Canada.

It would later be discovered that the Royal Canadian Mounted Police and the Canadian Army had concurred that there was no need to move the Japanese community while Canada was at war with Japan.

Noted Japanese Canadian activist and Citizenship Judge Art Miki has studied the history of that period.

"The pressure to dislocate the Japanese in British Columbia came, in fact, from provincial politicians who had feared that they might take over the province's economy," he explains.

"The war became a convenient excuse to divide and disperse the successful farmers and fishermen. Local politicians like then Liberal Member of Parliament Ian McKenzie actually ran on a platform of getting rid of the Japanese. It was McKenzie's personal recommendation to cabinet, not a vote in Parliament that was responsible for the whole fiasco that unfolded under The War Measures Act." Miki says.

Of course, it might not have happened if the Japanese had been allowed the same straightforward entitlement to Canadian citizenship as other immigrants.

But that was not the case, and one had only to remember the story of Yoshi Abe's father, Tomekichi Homma, to understand that. He had fought what was perhaps the first civil rights case in Canadian history over the right to vote.

The British Columbia government would allow Japanese nationals to apply for "naturalization" but it was granted at the whim of the government officials at whatever time the request was made. And even if a resident were naturalized, he or she still could not vote.

The voter's list had many uses apart from keeping track of people who were qualified to vote.

Government regulations said that, in order for a graduate of a professional school to be registered to practise that profession, s/he had to be on the voter's list. Keeping people off of the voter's list also kept them out of lucrative professions. A law enforcing those conditions had been passed around 1895.

Yoshi's father, the son of a Samurai family, and well educated, had decided to make himself a test case. He had put his name on the voters list in 1900.

When he was denied, he took his case to BC's provincial court and won; when the province challenged the decision, he took his case to Canada's Supreme Court and won again. Ultimately, the government of Canada took the case to the Privy Council in London, where the court sided with the government and against Tomekichi Homma.

It was a bitter defeat. Tomekichi remained a hero in his community, but the prolonged financial and emotional stress of prolonged court battles took its toll on his health.

The Citizenship Act passed in 1947 would eventually allow anyone born in Canada to be a citizen of the country. Japanese Canadians finally got to vote in 1948, an accomplishment Tomekichi Homma did not live to see.

Until then, they remained subject to discretionary treatment. Even before the events of Pearl Harbour they were required to carry color coded identity cards with photos and fingerprints, cards that had to be shown whenever requested.

After the war ended in 1945, people like Yoshimaru and Yoshi Abe were not allowed to return to their former homes around coastal BC. The policy of the federal government was to "disperse" them across central and eastern Canada. Those who refused to resettle in a new region of Canada would be sent back to Japan.

This was yet another form of homelessness.

Canada had taken everything.

Where to go?

Neither Abe-san nor Yoshi nor their two children would feel at home in Japan. Mr. Ito, a close friend of the family, had decided upon Manitoba, and the young family threw their lot in with him, but it was a wretched decision; Abe-san's father and mother would not come with them.

Abe-san told that part of his story at a much later rally for the redress of the Japanese in this country.

"Many years ago my father had worked at the CPR roundhouse in Moose Jaw and experienced an intolerably harsh winter there. At his age, he could not start over again. So in the summer of 1946, with broken hearts, my parents left Canada for Japan. They both died in 1961. I believe that the main reason (for their death) was their disappointment at the treatment they received from the government, and that they had lost faith in Canada.

"I visited Japan after an absence of sixty years. It was the first time for my wife. We went to Kyushu, where I was born and we visited my parents' grave. It was a very emotional experience, knowing that they too were victims of this "war" against the Japanese community in Canada.

"I strongly believe that these things should never happen to any citizens of this country."

When Abe-san, Yoshi and their three children arrived in Manitoba, they were confronted with another problem; Japanese were not permitted to live inside the city limits of Winnipeg. They were supposed to go to a farm, or to the outskirts of the city.

The internment camps had closed in 1945, but between 1941 and 1948, if Japanese families tried to buy property in Winnipeg, the government could seize it.

Somehow, the long years of constant insult to the body and to the spirit never took possession of Abe-san and his wife.

They eventually found a home and in it created an environment in which they and their children, Kazu, Yumi, Miki, Yuri and Amy could live in harmony with the all the events of their lives.

Abe-san had once dreamed of being an architect, but it was too late for that.

His first job in Manitoba was helping to construct the "pre-fab" homes that were so popular after the war. Then he decided he would put all the skills he had learned as a forced labourer in the camps to better use.

In 1953 he found a partner and together they created Fuji Builders a name that became synonymous with quality homes in Manitoba. Over the next thirty years, Fuji would also make a name for itself building most of the fine cottages in Ontario's famous Lake of the Woods region. Abe-san also participated in the design and building of Winnipeg's much admired Japanese consulate which was completed in 1977, the Japanese Canadian Centennial Year.

Abe-san was not content with a fine reputation for integrity as a builder and businessman. His personal struggles had left him a community-centred man with a deep respect for the importance of human rights.

Above all, he did not want the misery of what had happened to him to happen to his children, or to any other Canadian.

Living with the proud legacy of his father in law Tomekichi Homma, he also became a leader in educating both Japanese and non Japanese Canadians about the experiences of his people before, during and after World War Two.

Reliving his own experiences was deeply painful, but it was necessary. He helped explain the details of the internment camps by sharing his own story. He took his message to many diverse audiences.

When negotiations with the Federal Government for the redress of Canada's Japanese community finally began, he undertook another challenging task. He documented the progress of negotiations in The Outlook, the monthly Japanese language newspaper published by the Manitoba Japanese Canadian Citizens Association for more than fifty years.

Abe-san's friend and admirer Art Miki still marvels at Abe-san's contributions to The Outlook.

"When he started to write fifty years ago, and for a long time, he wrote it all by hand in Japanese calligraphy. Sometime he wrote an entire edition of the paper, which could take many days of working until after midnight."

Partly as a result of Abe-san's patient and committed efforts, about 200 Manitobans, along with other Canadians, finally received an apology and redress from the Government of Canada in 1988. Each one received a symbolic compensation of $21,000.

His life in Winnipeg, the city which initially refused him a home, has been a mutually rewarding experience, so much so that in 1991, the province of Manitoba awarded him the Prix Manitoba Award for outstanding contributions to the province's Japanese Canadian community, and for sharing Japanese art and culture with all Manitobans.

His modest house is a library of Japanese culture and history.

He continues to admire and collect ancient Japanese swords whose history and workmanship he can explain in minute detail. He also maintains an invaluable collection of Japanese wood block prints in the ancient style, a collection featured in a special exhibit when Japanese Canadians celebrated their Centennial in 1977.

Abe-san has served as president and then advisor to Manitoba's Buddhist Temple, helping to choose ministers and resolve whatever problems faced its members. He helped to found the city's Japanese Canadian Cultural Centre, and to design its traditional Japanese Garden which, at 91, he still visits and tends, when he is able.

Many Manitobans have passed through the incomparable gardens he has built for the Japanese pavilion at Folkorama since its inception.

Abe-san still loves the Winnipeg Blue Bombers, who have presented him with an honorary share in the football club because he hasn't missed one of their games in thirty years.

"The football is not unlike Go, the Japanese game which resembles Chess; I love following the strategies and counter strategies" he says. For years he used to pack up the whole family and take them to watch the Bombers practise at their Canada Packers site. He especially liked former Coach Bud Grant.

Wherever Abe-san is, there's a sketch pad nearby. During his time in the camps, he began sketching his own Christmas cards, and he's continued to do original pencil and ink drawings for other occasions. Much of his art features scenes of Winnipeg.

And he belongs still to the Haiku Club which he first joined when he lived in Canada's internment camps.

Winnipeg's Japanese Canadian community will publish the biography of Yoshimaru Abe in 2006.

Martin Bergen

. . . .

The Rhineland, Germany. June, 1950.

Martin Bergen is a strong, bright, healthy young man working in a steel mill. His family, from whom he has been separated by the ravages of World War Two, has found its way from a Mennonite Refugee camp near the Germany-Holland border to the safety and promise of a future in Canada.

Martin Bergen, though surrounded by many young men like himself, feels alone. He longs to join his family in Canada but he has been told – and told again, many times, that he cannot. Not now. Not ever.

He can't go to Canada because he is known to have been a soldier in the German army, and about such men Immigration Officials have good reason to assume the worst.

It will not be the last time Martin Bergen confronts the power of stereotypical thinking, but it will be, perhaps the most cruel.

The young man, just 23, had indeed served in the army of the Third Reich, but that is the least of his story.

Martin was a boy of 12 when the war broke out in September of 1939.

Life before that was hardly peaceful in Schoenhurst, a Mennonite village of Chortitza in Ukraine. Historic promises of religious freedom made to the religious sect by Katherine the Great had long ago turned to dust, and by Martin's time, Mennonite men disappeared routinely to work the coal mines of Siberia.

It was for that reason that Martin's stepfather always slept with a bag of food and tobacco under his bed, ready to accompany him on a surprise and possibly fatal journey.

Martin's childhood was marked not only by Stalinist purges, but by hunger and fear, and life turned more chaotic still when Germany broke the non-aggression pact it had signed with the Soviet Union in 1939, and pushed into the Russian steppes.

When he was 14, the German occupation began, and Martin's teenage energy was conscripted to dig never ending trenches at the Dneiper River. For a couple of years, Mennonites lived a hard, but less fearful existence, free, at least, of the night visits from the NKVD, the Soviet secret police.

When the German army was defeated at the siege of Stalingrad in 1943, it retreated and Russia's ethnic Germans fled the Ukraine by the thousands, a period still known to Mennonites as "The Great Trek."

Martin's family travelled in a foul, crowded boxcar to the first of their many refugee camps in (the former) Poland. Here the men, including boys as young as Martin, were told that Mennonites had the same duty to the Fatherland as ordinary Germans, and were drafted unceremoniously into Hitler's army.

As a Mennonite, Martin refused to carry a gun. It was common for German officers to make an example of difficult conscripts, and for this act of defiance, he might well have been shot, but miraculously, he was permitted to serve as a medic. He was trained in those duties and sent to the Western Front where he worked, often helplessly, on the battlefield with the wounded, the dead and the dying.

On April 30, 1945 he was among those soldiers who survived and surrendered to the Americans.

That would be was the beginning of three years as a prisoner of war, during which, many of the young soldiers, deprived of food and care, would wither and die.

"I remember many men were just lying there, waiting to die. Some gave up but I wanted to live," he says now.

"So if (the Americans) called for a work detail, I was the first in line."

He recalls also the kindness of one American guard on a work expedition in the nearby forest.

"The soldier knew we were desperately hungry. He went and shot a deer, brought it to us, skinned it and cut it into pieces which he gave us. We roasted it on sticks. And then we went to work.

That meant a lot to us. It meant there were still good people in the world."

He never forgot the impact of his enemy's kindness.

But things continued to worsen for his group of young prisoners of war when they were sent to France. There they would be mercilessly overworked and beaten regularly by Moroccan soldiers. There his weight fell to less than a hundred pounds, and his physical weakness landed him in the military hospital.

Life took another sharp turn and he found himself the object of French lessons so that he could be used to train recruits to the French Foreign Legion how to use weapons captured from the Germans. Ironically, they were the weapons he himself had refused to use.

In June of 1948, Martin Bergen was released at last from his prisoner of war status. He immediately tracked his family's whereabouts to Canada, and learned soon after that he was considered unfit for life in that country. A future lifetime behind the Iron curtain in Communist controlled East Germany loomed as a real possibility.

But believing deeply that he had done nothing wrong, Martin could not, would not accept his rejection. Having suffered many unbearable experiences as a conscript, and having done only what was necessary to stay alive, he insisted at every opportunity on a meeting with Immigration authorities from Canada.

They refused to see him. He tried again. And again.

When he finally got an interview with Canadian officials, providence offered him an unexpected advantage; his interviewing officer was French Canadian, and Martin was able to speak with him comfortably in French.

After an hour of talk about the war, the officer stood up and proclaimed, "You're the right man for Canada. We need guys like you there."

"I was not in Canada yet," he says," but it was a very big moment in my life."

That was 1950. It would be another three years before he got official permission to live in Canada. He would buy a ticket (with money borrowed from his relatives) and reach his parents' home in Winnipeg on Thanksgiving Day, 1953.

For the next year, he took any work that was offered to him, mostly

Painting, dry walling and general construction duties. On Thanksgiving Day, exactly a year after his arrival, the young tradesman took time out to get engaged to Ruth Spletzer, the lovely sister of a good friend. The couple had many things in common, among them that Ruth was also a refugee who had fought hard for her chance to come to Canada.

They married in February of 1955. They wanted what every young couple wants: a home, a family, and the ability to make their own way.

The couple had their only child, Miriam, in January of 1956. She was all the more precious because three more pregnancies ended in miscarriage.

Working in Winnipeg turned out to be a cut throat business.

There were lots of new contractors after the war; Martin would work for them, but sometimes, too often in fact, he didn't get to collect his pay.

Some employers were willing to cheat their workers to save money; some were honest and merely incompetent. Once, when he was actually forced to declare bankruptcy, he vowed he would never treat others in the same way.

At a time when his self-confidence might well have been shaken, Martin Bergen responded by taking a greater risk.

"I figured it might be easier being the builder. Then I could run the jobs and pay the crews myself."

In 1962, he found a friend and partner in Jake Letkemann, another immigrant with building and trades experience. Together, as the Marlborough Development Corporation, they would eventually change the face and the skyline of the City of Winnipeg.

It sounded like a grand company, but in the beginning, it actually operated out of the basement of the Bergen home with Ruth doing the filing, sorting and paperwork, when she wasn't busy with her daughter Miriam.

Early on, MDC learned the art of borrowing money and proceeded to use it to build small apartment blocks in Winnipeg and in the Selkirk area. One of their early ambitious projects was a one hundred suite building, the General Grant, in 1964. The equally ambitious Eiffel Towers followed soon after.

"My strategy was to know the people I worked with." Martin Bergen says. "I found people I thought were the absolute best at what they did, draftsmen, engineers, decorators, what have you, and I stuck with all of them from the very beginning."

It proved to be a solid business strategy.

By 1970, the Marlborough Development Corporation was

the biggest and best known builder of apartment buildings in the province, and Martin Bergen was ready to celebrate Manitoba's Centennial year with a special project: Granite House, an apartment exclusively for senior citizens on Henderson Highway in East Kildonan.

He told an interviewer then that "I built that for our mothers. We (post war Mennonite) immigrants all came to Canada with our mothers. Most of us had lost our fathers in that war. The families moved onto Ingersoll, Arlington, that area, close to the First Mennonite Church.

Then the children grew up, married, and moved out to North Kildonan, East Kildonan and so on. My mother had a two bedroom house and she stayed in that house by herself. So I said, I'm going to build Granite House. I'm going to make small suites."

Mother said, "In our house you do not sit on the bed, the bed is to sleep on." So they had to be one bedroom, (not bachelor) suites. I figured the project out so Mother and her friends could afford to move in there…my

Mother and so many others were very happy there."

The place filled up so quickly that he and Letkemann built another

Senior's housing apartment on Henderson, the Fort Agassiz.

Both buildings are still one hundred percent occupied. The man who went on to become known as "the King of Winnipeg Apartment Developers" still considers this his finest achievement.

In 1972, less than twenty years after he landed in Winnipeg, Martin Bergen found himself in a place he could never have imagined: on a billboard produced by Canada Manpower and Immigration.

His picture was also featured on a poster in transit buses and in every airport in Canada.

"In 1953," the billboard read, "Canada welcomed Martin Bergen. In 1972, Martin Bergen is saying thanks by giving

Canadians employment."

It went on to detail that the Marlborough Development Corporation employed 75 people in winter, and 200 people in summer. About the same time, he got a phone call from the immigration officer who had once interviewed him in Germany and allowed him into this country.

"He told me people were complaining that they were letting too many foreigners into the country, and they were taking jobs away from Canadians He was fighting back by talking about guys like me."

But not everybody admired his Martin Bergen's success.

By now he had a reputation for being a big builder with a stubborn streak, determined to do things his own way. And by then, "I was so accustomed to opposition, it didn't bother me much."

Martin's property management company, Edison Rental Agency, maintained excellent relations with the tenants in his buildings. For years, every tenant received a Christmas present.

There was a rough patch, too, still talked about as "the sign war."

Like many post war Mennonites who had suffered under communism, Martin Bergen was a staunch Conservative supporter. To people of his generation, socialism was a step in the wrong direction. During one of Manitoba's provincial elections, Martin saw far too many signs going up on the balconies and in the windows of his apartments in support of Ed Schreyer's New Democrats. He issued an edict he hoped would put a stop to it: No more political signs on balconies.

Instead, it ignited a revolution, and he was forced to back down.

"We sure lost that one," he says. "Now anybody can put any sign they please."

He was often pictured in media at the centre of one heated controversy or another.

"For example, when I got the idea to build the Castle on

the Seine," some people told me outright that I was crazy!"

In 1985, he was tired of putting up merely efficient buildings, and he still enjoyed his memories of ancient European architecture. Out of those combined feelings came "The Castle" on Niakwa Road, a six story medieval style apartment block featuring turrets, columns, and statues all imported from Europe and fronted by Manitoba Tyndall stone.

It became something of a Winnipeg landmark, and Martin Bergen thought for awhile that his castle might be his swan song.

It wasn't.

Just a year later, in an era marked by famed revolving restaurants in Seattle, Calgary and Toronto, the developer brought one to Winnipeg. It was part of a $65 million project, Fort Garry Place, a three tower complex built next to the venerable Fort Garry Hotel and overlooking the Assiniboine River on its way to meet the Red.

The project was furiously debated, but Martin Bergen got his way and the Royal Crown is one of the city's favourite restaurants, especially on New Years Eve and Canada Day when Manitobans seem to want to see or show off a panoramic view of the entire city of Winnipeg.

Fort Garry Place may have been Martin Bergen's last building project,

But it was not the end of his career as a philanthropist and community builder.

"I learned early in the development business that the best way to secure the co-operation of other people is always to offer something in return. Nothing wrong with that; makes perfect sense. But there are other times when you should just give something because it's needed, and because you can."

And there was always the lingering gratitude he felt to Canada for accepting him and allowing him to re-unite with his family when he was young and more or less penniless. It was not coincidental that his buildings always flew large Canadian flags.

His generosity had always been commensurate with his means. Back in 1971, parents in North Kildonan were intent on providing their children with a skating rink. Fund raising was slow and difficult, and at the depths of their neighbourhood's discouragement, Martin and his partner Jake Letkemann not only built their arena, they paid for it as well.

He came to the rescue again in 1979 when it came to his attention that local parents of disabled children were trying to find a place they could use for respite purposes. He remodelled an older home on Henderson Highway for them, and later added a two story residence on the property. SPIKE (Special People In Kildonan East) is still providing a place where overburdened parents can leave their children for short periods, confident that they are safe and cared for.

There was also the student residence he built for Providence Bible College in Otterbourne, Manitoba. He was also a major contributor to Concordia Village, a retirement project still under construction.

Some of Martin Bergman's philanthropy is well known, such as his family's two million dollar contribution to the St Boniface Hospital and Research Centre's HeartCare campaign in 2003. It will help provide a cardiovascular centre of excellence to open in Winnipeg in 2006. The campaign will also help to fund a research partnership between the hospital and the world-renowned Mayo Clinic in Rochester, Minnesota.

Many of his contributions are much less known to the public, one of them being the Movement Centre of Manitoba, a support centre for people living with neuro-motor injuries, many of them children. Previously the parents of such children had to take them out of the province for special therapy. Thanks to the generosity of Martin Bergen, they have now established a permanent local home designed and equipped for the needs of their programs in a large space on Henderson Highway.

Some of his other activities had nothing to do with benevolence at all; they were just things he wanted to do.

When the Berlin wall fell in November of 1989, the event had special significance for Martin Bergen.

"How could I not pay attention to that? I might have lived my entire life as a prisoner on the other side!" he says. Two of his brothers in law did just that.

He did more than pay attention. He imported a slab of the fallen wall to Winnipeg. He brokered a deal in which East Germany agreed to send it in exchange for used medical equipment no longer needed by Concordia Hospital.

"Us old guys know what happened, but the kids need to know too.

They should have something to look at so they can ask questions."

Manitoba's very own slab of the historic wall eventually found its way to Steinbach, where it now sits outside the Mennonite Heritage Museum.

His daughter Miriam manages most of Martin's affairs these days and Martin takes every chance he gets to golf. "I used to think it was a stupid game, but I find I like walking the course" he says.

He also enjoys the daily company of his long-time buddies at a local coffee shop.

He rarely talks about his accomplishments or his services to his community, although he certainly could. He provided almost 6,000 apartment homes for Winnipeggers, and he's received the Canada 125 Medal, the Queen's Golden Jubilee Medal and Manitoba's highest award, the Order of the Buffalo Hunt.

When a researcher for the St Boniface Hospital asked him how he would like to be remembered, his answer was unqualified.

"Just that I was honest, and worked hard."

Dr. Naranjan Dhalla

. . . .

Dr. Naranjan Dhalla, world renowned scholar in matters of the heart, considers himself a man of less than average intelligence.

"I can't even hammer a nail into a wall," he confides with regret. "The computer is no friend of mine."

He considers himself a comparatively unaccomplished man, too.

"It's only the others who help me do things."

These are sincere beliefs, and they are consistent with a profound humility which he learned at an early age at the hands of his father and an assortment of very strict teachers with very high expectations.

Truth be told, and Naranjan Dhalla is pre-occupied with truth, the good professor has very little to be humble about.

Few lives are as widely celebrated as his, and certainly not while they are still unfolding.

When Canadian scientists decided in 2001 to name their "Miracle Men", the twelve colleagues from all over the world they considered to be living legends for their contributions to medical breakthroughs, Naranjan Dhalla's name was on the list.

The Canadian Medical Association awarded him their Medal of Honour. His work has been cited in parliament, and he has been named to the Order of Canada, not to mention more than one hundred other awards and honorary distinctions, many of them international.

He accepts them, he appreciates and he is grateful, but glory never goes to his head. Although he is essentially a cerebral man – a scientist, a teacher, a visionary and an extraordinary promoter-he remains a man for whom the human heart is supreme.

"My whole existence is an experiment with the truth," he has said many times, "especially the truth about our lack of knowledge of heart function and heart disease."

His passion to uncover the secrets of the heart has saved a large, though precisely unknown number of lives, brought millions of dollars into Manitoba's economy and, at least in terms of medical science, turned the "brain drain" into a "brain gain" for this province.

Born in 1936 in Ghanieke, Punjab, India into a progressive Sikh family, he never really expected to leave, much less to become the internationally applauded scientific researcher he is today.

"I was not born very rich, handsome, a star athlete, a great student or clever orator. Name anything wonderful; it was not me. But I didn't know this because I was the son of the most important man in my village, a man who succeeded at business with a grade four education. We had the best of everything.

Awareness did not come until I was about eighteen that the world was full of important men, and I would have to find a place for myself, by myself."

It was this discovery that would shape and direct my future, a will to be the best at whatever I chose to do".

His first job was as a researcher in a women's medical college in New Delhi in the department of pharmacology. It was here that a fanatically methodical teacher, Dr. C.L Malhotra taught him the basics of research.

"He was so thorough, he wouldn't trust facts from his own mother, if she'd dared to offer them. He had to see everything with his own eyes." He also credits another teacher, Dr. P. K. Das for the impossibly high standards that have served him so well over the last 45 years.

He finished his undergraduate studies in 1956, in an era when North American influence in medical sciences was growing, and his mentor, Dr. Das suggested graduate study in America. Dhalla applied both at the University of Toronto and the University of Pennsylvania.

"They both accepted me, but Toronto's acceptance arrived one day after that of Pennsylvania. I was very interested in Canada, but it was too late."

If he had gone to Toronto, would he ever have found his way to Winnipeg?

"Who knows? I didn't really care where I was then. I just wanted to learn. But still, I suspect Manitoba was my destiny." he says.

Dhalla finished a Master's Degree in Science at the University of Pennsylvania and a Ph D in pharmacology at the University of Pittsburgh. and moved to take a position at St. Louis University.

"I was assistant professor to a unique individual there, Dr. Robert Olson. From him I learned that it was not enough to love and respect science, you must also promote it enthusiastically so others will feel the same way. Dr. Olson taught me the best way, by example, how to do that. He also modelled the qualities of leadership which could distinguish an outstanding career from an ordinary one."

After a couple of years at St Louis, Naranjan Dhalla met

the man who would change his future, and the future of the University of Manitoba in the field of heart research.

In Dr. Dhalla's opinion, Arnold Naimark was "the most clever academic recruiter God ever sent to earth. This fellow described some jobs available in the physiology department at the U of M, and he made the future sound dazzling."

"Everyone was saying to me, "Don't go, Dhalla, don't go. There's nothing there."

"But this recruiter was young, he had vision, he was polished. Without even seeing Winnipeg, I told him I would come, if I could bring seven of my brightest students and Fellows with me."

To his surprise and delight, Naimark agreed. The decision would be the first tentative step in building Manitoba into a medical Mecca for cardiovascular research. Dhalla and the seven Fellows he insisted on bringing would become Manitoba's first experimental heart research team.

"I was still missing India and my roots in Punjab" Dhalla says." My family was there, but both research and bureaucracy were different there; there were simply no equivalent opportunities."

He arrived in Winnipeg in August of 1968 and started off as an assistant professor of physiology in the Faculty of Medicine.

He was already in love with the mysteries of the heart.

In the early sixties, cardiovascular illness carried a 62 % fatality rate (a figure which has been reduced to slightly more than 37% in 2005). Few imagined then the breakthroughs that would occur in the lead up to the end of the 20th century.

Dhalla cites them with the ease of a grocery list:

"In the 60s, there came beta blockers; in the 70s, calcium antagonists; in the 80s, ACE inhibitors and the 90s, angiotension antagonists; each another little step in unlocking the puzzle of the heart.

I have been very lucky to see these things develop in a

beautiful order."

Inspired and excited by new possibilities, Naranjan Dhalla was to make several hugely significant contributions to the advancement of cardiac understanding at the University of Manitoba, contributions that would reverberate around the globe, especially in the West where roughly half of all deaths are due to coronary disease caused by the heart's reduced capacity to pump blood through the hum an body.

But one dedicated researcher, no matter how promising, has limited effectiveness.

The friendship of two men in Manitoba greatly inspired him.

He considers Dr. Henry Friesen, who replaced Arnold Naimark as his boss at the University of Manitoba, one of the great men in Canadian medicine, and when they worked closely together, he challenged Dhalla not to rest on accomplishments, but push himself even harder.

Dr. Robert Beamish was the first man to think aggressively about Winnipeg as a centre of cardiac expertise, one who saw in Dhalla a man with similar ideas

"He was a completely selfless man, a spiritual as well as an intellectual example, and he enshrined the value of ethics both in science and in life. His death was a great loss to Manitoba. I still look over at his empty office and miss his presence there."

Naranjan Dhalla knew that if he wanted to be successful in the fight against heart disease, he would need to build an entire community of people working toward the same goal.

"I must admit that part of my success has been due to people in Winnipeg who have been kind to me. My friend Ivan Berkowitz, for example, has helped me understand this city, and has contributed greatly to my peace of mind and satisfaction in working here."

His brilliance as a researcher was accompanied by a second and rare gift; the ability to bring people with different interests together and inspire them to work as one family. He believed that a multi-disciplinary approach (looking at heart disease from the molecular, biochemical, physiological and pharmacological perspective) could and would produce more significant results than other approaches.

Following Arnold Naimark's example, Dhalla would recruit more than twenty ambitious young researchers from around the world.

In 1978, ten years after he arrived in Winnipeg, with the support of the Medical Research Council, his group evolved into a Centre for Excellence for cardiovascular work in Canada. This allowed him to recruit more expertise and faculty members. And in 1987, the establishment of the St Boniface Research Centre which would eventually give him an opportunity and a place to locate the now famous Institute for Cardiovascular Science (ICS).

Today the ICS is a joint Institute of the University of Manitoba and St. Boniface General Hospital. In 1994, the ICS received a huge grant from the Medical Research Council. Since then, the group has focused on several aspects of coronary disease, especially the repair of heart muscle tissue, injuries caused by high blood pressure and cholesterol at a molecular level, and the prevention of the causes of restricted blood flow.

"When you decide to test the mysteries of nature, you have to accept that you may fail. But you must remember always the lessons of failure. Failure is a wise teacher, so you must plan, observe keenly and participate fully, no matter how your work is going. It is imperative to remember you personally have no control over outcome."

And sometimes, after what looks like endless failure, comes success.

Under Dr. Dhalla's leadership, his team at the Institute of Cardiovascular Sciences has made exciting progress around the blockage of the coronary artery and congestive heart failure.

In 2004, the *Medical Post*, the newspaper of the Canadian

medical establishment, saluted Dr. Dhalla and his lab at the University of Manitoba for their outstanding success in those two areas.

He and his team have shown that a particular kind of sub-cellular change causes the heart dysfunction in congestive heart failure and chronic diabetes. They were also able to show what induces this destructive subcellular change and what operations might prevent it. This represents a new concept explaining the molecular basis of heart problems in a wide range of heart disease.

The *Post* also paid tribute to the achievements of Dhalla and his team on stress-induced heart disease and the regulation of calcium. The understanding of the oxidation process in the damage to heart cells was a big step forward in cardiovascular science; it has allowed Dhalla and his team to discover two new procedures for reducing arrhythmias (irregular heart beat) and death due to heart attacks.

Dhalla is known not only as a researcher, but as a medical writer. He has published more than 650 papers and 40 books on heart research. He played a critical role in establishment and development of the prestigious Canadian Journal of Cardiology. He's also editor–in-chief of Molecular and Cellular Biochemistry, an influential international journal published in Boston and printed in Holland.

Of all his accomplishments, his discovery and development of a new drug known as MC-1 may excite him the most.

MC-1 is a naturally occurring molecule in the human body, one which appears to treat blockages of the coronary artery and congestive heart failure It has so far gone successfully through two drug trials, and if its success continues to market, may cut the incidence of heart attack in human beings by 31%, possibly more.

"The possibilities are staggering, it was a breathtaking journey," Dhalla says," but you will never meet anyone who thinks Naranjan Dhalla is an entrepreneur or a business man. No, no, no, not at all!"

But here his genius for networking came into play.

Contemplating the challenges of advancing his discovery, he contacted well known Manitoba bio-tech developer Dr. Albert Friesen, the creator of several health product companies, who found the prospects of MC-1 equally exciting.

Together they licensed the compound, obtained the patents and co-founded a company called Medicure to oversee its development. Medicure has provided jobs for more than fifty people, many of them top researchers Both the university and St Boniface Hospital are partners with Medicure and stand to gain significantly if the new drug fulfills its promise.

"This could be a multi-billion dollar enterprise," Dr. Dhalla laughs, and typically, gives most of the credit to Dr. Friesen and to the University of Manitoba and St. Boniface General Hospital for supporting his work.

In his view, the money will be less important than the legacy of improved cardiovascular health.

"It may be part of my destiny to contribute this particular piece of the puzzle."

Although he is a Sikh who wore a turban for a good part of his life, he does not identify with the idea of any conventional religion.

Naranjan Dhalla is, however, a deeply spiritual man and a big believer in destiny.

As he sees it, every human being is a miniature copy of the universe.

He once explained the human body to a graduate student newspaper as "a level of organization with a distinctive belt of charge and a signal like the signal of an electrocardiogram; unique. Every human being has a halo or belt of charges that we are unable to detect, but disturbance in this belt result in a person getting sick, crying, laughing, etc. The sun, moon and stars within the universe all influence this belt of charges to a degree we still do not understand.

A strong pull of influence exists, nonetheless. So you can

see the similarities between charges in a human body and charges in the universe, and how they can influence each other. So the God factor of religion is of paramount importance."

But for Dr.Dhalla, "The basic element of religion is respect and service for others, and I dedicate myself to this...I believe God lives within everybody, and thus respecting other person's viewpoints and understanding their nature can make people very religious. This is how I see people should be. For me, my work is my religion."

The work goes on, and in Dr. Dhalla's view, success is a mere by-product of the willingness to serve.

It's that willingness to serve that helps to explain how his presence sometimes transforms his surroundings.

Consider his simple membership in the International Society for Heart Research, a powerful organization of experts which started in Dubrovnik in 1968 and now has a large membership of cardiologists, heart surgeons and cardiovascular scientists. He helped to shape it as a progressive forum where cardiovascular research from around the world could be exchanged.

Because of his "willingness to serve" the ISHR (he became its secretary-general and president) as well as to serve Manitoba, the world congress of the ISHR came to Winnipeg in 2001. It attracted almost 2000 cardiovascular researchers from 72 countries around the globe, reinforcing Winnipeg as a leader in that field.

The conference lasted a week and brought several million dollars to the city. Many people saw the event as the most impressive international event since the great success of the 1999 Pan American games.

"In my own little way," he told a Winnipeg newspaper, "I wanted to let people see that the very best can come here. That's what happened."

Small wonder that the city of Winnipeg has put a bust of Dr. Naranjan Dhalla in its Citizens Hall of Fame in the city's lush Assiniboine Park.

A mistake, Dhalla chuckles, another mystery!

What he remembers about that part of his life is that the sculptor, Eva Stubbs, complained that she could not sculpt the twinkle in his eyes.

After he retired from the executive of the International Society for Heart Research, Dhalla turned his attention to the formation of a new academy of cardiovascular sciences with its permanent head office in Winnipeg. Its mission is to promote the education of not only professionals but lay people in the ways of the heart, and to recognize cardiovascular achievement around the world.

"Heart disease and heart attacks are still the number one killer. My idea is to get news about it to the public. New discoveries which can save lives should be shared much faster than they are."

As much as the distinguished scholar of the heart has learned about the heart from his laboratory, the most difficult lesson was a deeply personal one.

In the autumn of 2003 his son Sam died without warning at the untimely age of 42. The cause was diagnosed as Sudden Death, a condition in which the heart simply stops. Unlike a heart attack, in which a regular heartbeat may be recovered, there is no heart beat at all. The loss of his son left him not only bereft but with an overwhelming sense of helplessness and inadequacy, with an even deeper sense of humility than before.

It also caused him to think about the future and where he might still do his most useful work.

"To go back to destiny, I have come here, and I have realized over the years the suffering of native Canadians because of diabetes. Aboriginal people experience the cardiovascular problems caused by diabetes in great numbers. I am thinking that may be why the universe has brought me here and I am asking myself what I can do for them. It might take the rest of my life and several more millions of dollars, but you know many great things can happen if only you promise yourself that they will."

As those plans formulate, he will continue to mentor students, the importance of which, he says, simply cannot be exaggerated.

In his zeal to recognize and promote young scientists, he has established endowments from his own consulting fees for ten awards at the St Boniface Hospital Research Centre and a further eight at the University of Manitoba.

"It's a small way of saying I was here, I had the chance to serve."

Dr. Dhalla will also continue to research and write and, he hopes, grow closer still to his family. He has four other grown children.

"My children, Sonny, Sonia, Vikram and Romel have developed into fine people with exceptional leadership abilities. They are my real strength because they are true friends. My wish to put a trustworthy example in front of them has saved me from making many a silly mistake I might otherwise have made. They, along with my brother Kalwant (Ken), a noted Punjabi poet and my brother in law Joginder Shamsher inspire and challenge me to keep learning valuable things well outside the realm of science.

"It is my only regret that my work has caused such loneliness for my wife, Ranjit, who has done so much for me and for our family all by herself. Science owes as much to her as to me.

I am still searching for balance in my life. I can't even play a game.

I hardly watch the Indian movies I love so much. My son has bought me an exercise bike ten years ago and still I am not using it!

Many people have honoured me over my career, but I tell you I do not deserve such admiration. The idea that anyone achieves anything by himself is total nonsense!"

He says this with complete conviction.

But about Dr. Naranjan Dhalla, the world, and especially Canada, thinks differently.

Dr. Joseph Du

. . . .

Dr. Joseph Du is King of the Castle now.

After 34 years of living in the same modest house in which he and his wife Jeannine raised their four children, they are settled in a comfortable high rise apartment, the windows of which look out on the grey stone turrets of Winnipeg's venerable Fort Garry Hotel.

"My grandchildren call it Harry Potter's house" he says, eyes twinkling with amusement. "I guess that makes me Harry Potter's neighbour."

Dr. Joseph Du retired from his medical practice in 2002. Though he's still actively absorbed in civic life, especially the affairs of Manitoba's Asian community, it's a somewhat slower, softer life than any of his previous lives, and there have been many.

Joe Du, hungry kid and war orphan.

Joe Du, refugee, lonely student, struggling doctor.

Not to forget Joe Du-to-the-Rescue of people in need, and Joe Du of the North.

And of course, there's Joe Du, unofficial diplomat, trader in polar and panda bears, close personal friend of Rong Rong and Ching Ching,

He was born in Laokay near Haiphong in northern Vietnam in 1933, the youngest son in an ethnic Chinese family of eleven children. His brothers survived their poverty and war torn childhood, but his sisters did not. All five of them died, the last at just nine months of age of complications from pneumonia.

"I was only a kid…maybe nine years old, but I just knew those babies didn't get the medical care they needed. I knew they should have lived, like me. That may have been my first thought of being a doctor who could look after children."

He wasn't much older when, during world war two, an American bomb was dropped on Haiphong's Chinatown.

It was meant for the Japanese invaders, but it fell on the building where Joe's father loved to play Mah Jong with his friends and colleagues.

"We (my family and I) searched for him in the remains of a six story building for a week. What we found was unidentifiable, but we knew we had found him when we recognized his watch and his socks."

Joe's mother was left a widow with five children and no means to raise them.

The Chinese were a powerful force in Vietnam and ran their own elementary and high schools. They offered scholarships to ethnic families like the Du's and Joe, who attended primary school during the American blockade of Vietnam, still remembers walking to school every morning through starving bodies on the street.

"Everyone was hungry. There was no food, no rice. The people in the streets were skin and bones, some dead, some dying. There was nothing to do for them; you just had to keep walking." Those memories haunt him to this day, especially when he sees footage of modern day Iraq.

And when one war ended, another began.

Although the Japanese had surrendered in Vietnam and the Chinese returned to occupy their former possession in the north, negotiations in Europe bequeathed the area to France. The Chinese refused to retreat.

"More bloodshed and homelessness for the children, always the children suffering," he comments.

In 1954, the Geneva conference divided the country into North and South Vietnam, and the ethnic Chinese were faced with an awesome choice; a future in Communist China or in Taiwan.

Joe, who dreamed of being a paediatrician in a place like Hong Kong some day, took the first refugee flight to Taipei. The government there was promising to educate a new generation of students who arrived from Vietnam.

He had to leave his mother behind. She was crying.

He was seventeen years old.

"I can recall also the cargo plane I left on, full of students, about a hundred of us, and we sat on the floor with our knapsacks or small bags during the eight hour flight."

"I landed there with exactly $50 US, young, homesick and speaking only Cantonese, whereas the language of Taiwan was Mandarin. Not only that – the medical texts were almost exclusively in English. I spent so many long, long nights with dictionaries. No family, no friends.

It was six months before I understood what was going on around me.

On my first Chinese New Year, everything was closed and I celebrated by myself with powdered milk and cookies."

He still winces at the memory.

He graduated from Taiwan's national medical school in 1961. Of eight classmates with whom he had started medical training, seven had dropped out. The new doctor had also learned everything there was to know about living an alien life in a country that is not home.

Still hoping to do his doctoring in Hong Kong, he was obliged to get accreditation in a Commonwealth country. Australia was a possibility, but it had a reputation then for a nasty brand of aggressive racism. Canada, on the other hand, was perceived to be a country which compensated for a cold climate with a warm attitude.

Joe Du was 28 years old when he chose Canada.

The Grey Nuns' Hospital in Regina was the first to offer him a job: a junior internship. After the crowded landscape of Vietnam and Taiwan, he was taken aback on his arrival in the small prairie city. It appeared to him to be deserted.

"Where was everybody? There were so few people! I decided there must be a curfew, or maybe martial law."

He remembers practising his English at night in the hospital's senior wards and by helping the nurses out even when he was off duty.

He was happy and full of hope. Busy too; unknown to him, he'd arrived during the first rebellious days of Medicare. The doctors of Saskatchewan were on strike and the interns were doing everything.

For a long time, life was a blur of work and sleep.

"Racism? If there was any, there was no time for that."

Joe Du next moved to Winnipeg to wait for an opening in the Children's hospital, and during a stint at the Misericordia hospital, met the woman with whom he would share the rest of his life.

He remembers little fuss or resistance to the prospect of an inter-racial marriage into Jeannine's French Canadian family. The big issue rather, was whether he was Catholic enough to be married at St Boniface Cathedral.

The Church agreed to investigate his Catholic credentials, but cautioned it might take quite a lot of time.

One day, while the couple was watching a tennis match at the Winnipeg Canoe Club, someone tapped Joe on the back and launched into a Chinese conversation.

"I turned around and I couldn't believe it; it was Father

Bruyère, the priest from my church in Taiwan. He was back home in St. Boniface!"

Father Bruyère put in a good word for Joe. The Church dropped its investigation, and the couple married amid much joy in St. Boniface Cathedral in 1964.

In 1967, Joe Du became a citizen of Canada, and unlike his celebration in Taiwan, this time he was surrounded by family and friends.

"It was a special time. I felt, now I really belong. Canada is my home."

In 1968, he landed a coveted job at the Winnipeg Clinic and settled down to the practise of everyday medicine and the kind of healing that had interested from his earliest days in Vietnam. It was the first time the prestigious clinic, one of the best in western Canada, accepted a member of a visible minority into its ranks.

About the same time, his life took another unimaginable turn.

It turned north.

Some medical friends, his colleague Dr. Doug Kerr among them, asked him to join them in their medical outreach to aboriginal communities in Northern Manitoba. He and his wife had two young children by then, but with memories of Vietnam still clear and with Jeannine's support, he felt compelled to say yes.

Manitoba was still a year away from Medicare and neither the government nor the natives could pay the bills then. The medical volunteers all went up, usually three or four times a year, for about a week at a time, just because they were needed.

Everything about the north was a shock.

"Just getting there took my breath away. I remember my first flight in a government Cessna 180, just me and the pilot in this flimsy little tube. He saw me looking down at the lakes and endless trees and he could read my mind. He said, don't worry, Joe, if we go missing they'll look for us right away!"

"The first time we flew into Norway House, I thought I was going to die. They didn't have a landing strip then and we were in a ski plane and we landed too hard. I looked out the window and saw it was underwater. But the gods were in a good mood that day – we didn't drown. We surfaced and we carried on as usual."

Conditions in the northern nursing stations were painfully primitive.

"They were still using two way phones from world war two, the kind where you had to say Roger, Roger, Over, Over, that kind of thing. I waited years for a paediatric examining table. And there was always a crowd because everyone knew when we were coming, and they'd be lined up waiting, like for a show."

Over time, he and the other doctors would be paid for their medical services in the north but it was common for them to see twice as many patients in one day as they would in Winnipeg. The trips were always physically and emotionally draining.

The financial sacrifice paled compared to the risk of travel, and the separation from family.

"You went up never knowing when you'd get back. It was especially hard on Jeannine. It was there I learned the meaning of the phrase "weather permitting.""

And it was tough to see so much suffering; suicides, domestic brutality, fetal alcohol damaged infants.

"Northern peoples were abandoned for so long, and change so slow in coming; for example, it was years before the water on northern reserves was fluoridated.

We visiting doctors couldn't do that much, but we felt better for staying with it." he says now.

Joe Du continued to travel to and work with Manitoba's northern communities for 33 years and doesn't regret one day of it.

Around 1975, he found himself in a totally different but

equally essential and unexpected kind of activism.

When he had arrived in Winnipeg in the late sixties, there were only a handful of Asian families here. Those numbers were increasing and the increase brought new issues into play, a fact which became very clear to him when he attended the first National Conference of Chinese Canadians in Vancouver that year. He led a delegation of eight Winnipeggers.

A new crisis loomed in 1979.

American troops had withdrawn from Vietnam in 1975, leaving a fearful population behind them. In 1979, the phenomenon known as "the boat people" exploded. Waves of people rushed to escape the consequences of the retreat.

The first group of 32 refugees from Vietnam were scheduled to arrive at the Winnipeg Airport, and the Canadian Red Cross and Canada's Immigration authorities approached Joe Du for help.

They arrived in various stages of shock and fear, many of them unable to communicate with anyone but him. They reminded Joe of the sorrowful and anxious young man who had once landed in a cargo plane at a Taiwan airport.

They needed food, shelter, medical and dental care.

"First we had to sort out family groups – all we had to go by was a faxed list of names. Then we had to look at immediate medical needs.

Many of the children suffered from what we call "bombed-out mouths", having lived a hand-to-mouth existence in camps, with few opportunities for dental hygiene. Kids as young as 18 months had developed dental problems and needed attention right away.

Drawing on his personal network of medical colleagues, Joe co-ordinated as much help as he could manage.

A little known legacy of the "Boat People Era" was that Manitoba gained a huge amount of medical expertise.

Among the refugees there were more than twenty Vietnamese doctors who had lost everything, even their personal identification, and had no idea how to prepare for a new medical career in Canada. Dr. Jim Morrison, then Registrar of the College of Physicians and Surgeons of Manitoba naturally sent them to Dr. Joe Du.

Joe, working with the College and with the University of Manitoba's faculty of medicine, helped to develop a screening and retraining program which would enable the doctors to upgrade and find quick placement as interns.

His refugee retraining program would also come to the aid of refugee doctors from El Salvador, Poland and Romania.

In the next decade, Winnipeg's Asian population mushroomed to 20,000 people, a substantial number of them traumatized, desperately increasing the need for housing and social services.

Once again, he was compelled and willing to be in the vanguard of problem solving. He worked overtime trying to explain the problems of the newcomers to several levels of government, especially authorities in then Immigration Minister Lloyd Axworthy's Core Area Initiative.

In the post war years, as families prospered, there had been a residential exodus from Chinatown to other areas of Winnipeg, and much of its previous communal character and "livability" had declined considerably.

Relentless pressure from its leadership, including Joe Du would turn it around.

In 1987, the Chinese community applauded when the first phase of Winnipeg's China Town, the King Street Bridge, the multi-purpose Dynasty Building, Harmony Housing, and the Chinese Gardens were completed.

Joe Du's work as liason between Asian and non Asian people would lead him to other responsibilities: to service as advisor to the provincial and federal Ministers of Health on multicultural matters, the executive of the Council for Canadian Unity, to the presidency of Winnipeg's International Centre, among others. He was one of those who initiated the Manitoba Academy of Chinese Studies, where both Canadians and Asian youth could learn the languages of Asia.

His experiences a multicultural negotiator would also help him bring one of the most popular and successful events to Winnipeg that the city has ever seen.

Enter Rong Rong and Ching Ching, the Pandas who stole Winnipeg's heart in 1989.

Enter Joe Du, tight rope walker and acrobat.

During a stopover at the Calgary airport, Joe had learned from a wall poster that a pair of panda Bears direct from China would be one of that city's special attractions at the Winter Olympics there in 1987.

Why not bring them to Winnipeg for a couple of months before their return to China?

After all, in the spirit of progressive politics, he and his likeminded colleague at city hall, Mayor Bill Norrie had been carefully cultivating relations between Winnipeg and China.

Early in 1987, Joe had heard from his northern network that there were a few polar bear cubs available for export. He had managed to send a pair of playful young cubs from Churchill to the Taiwan Zoo.

He facilitated the gift of a second pair intended for Cheng Du (now a sister city to Winnipeg) but a crafty zookeeper in Beijing had cleverly hijacked the cubs for his own city, requiring another pair of the popular animals for Cheng Du.

Watching the exchange of polar bears and panda bears and sensing an opportunity for a diplomatic coup, China's ambassador to Canada asked Joe to mediate with the Zoo in Taiwan; he recruited Joe to go to Taiwan and convince them to accept pandas from communist China.

"It was like the ping pong diplomacy that preceded Nixon's formalization of relations between the US and China, except this time it was pandas."

And this time, the political positions of China and Taiwan were too entrenched; the strategy didn't work.

The children of Taiwan still can't see a panda at their zoo, but in 1989, though told many times it was impossible, Winnipeg welcomed the loan of Rong Rong and Ching Ching, the pandas who stole the show for the entire summer of that year.

Over a million people visited the pandas, bringing huge revenues to the city and province.

"If we wanted those pandas now, we'd have to sign a ten year contract at a rental fee of a million dollars a year. It just wouldn't happen!" Only two other cities in Canada have enjoyed the pandas – Calgary and Toronto.

Joe Du's interest and energy were never restricted to his own community. His early experiences had taught him that suffering is no respecter or race, culture, or ethnicity.

"The more we understand each other's history, the more we will come together and build stronger communities with more secure human rights and racial harmony." he says.

In the winter of 1998, he happened to read in a Vancouver Chinese newspaper about an upcoming exhibit at that city's Holocaust Museum. It was based on the heroic acts of Dr. Feng Shan Ho of China and Chiune Sugihara of Japan during the holocaust.

The men had bravely and quietly issued visas which allowed thousands of Jews to escape Europe for the safety of Shanghai, and four Winnipeg families were among the 18,000 people who were able to live there during the Second World War.

It was a little known story, and Joe thought Manitobans should get a chance to hear it. He brought it to the attention of the Jewish Heritage Centre of Western Canada in Winnipeg, and a first-time collaboration was born between Winnipeg's Jewish, Japanese and Chinese communities.

"The Shanghai Connection" exhibit opened to enthusiastic crowds soon after in Winnipeg.

The director of the Jewish centre told local media then that the two diplomats at the centre of the exhibit "demonstrated the power of the individual to transcend cultural differences, fear and circumstance to act selflessly and compassionately on behalf of fundamental human rights."

She might well have said the same thing about Dr. Joe Du and his life in Canada.

Dr. Joe Du has been honoured with the Order of the Buffalo (1997), The Order of Manitoba (2003), The Order of Canada (1985) and appointed International Friendship Ambassador (Cheng Du, 1997)

He and his wife Jeannine have four grown children: Alexander, Audrey, Jennifer and Michelle. They have eight grandchildren.

Arnold Frieman

. . . .

Arnold Frieman, the visionary businessman who founded a hugely successful electronic business in Winnipeg, came here in 1951 because he loved cowboys.

He was 21 when he left Norway, and headed for a job at the Canadian Marconi Company in Windsor, Ontario. On the voyage over, however, he struck up a conversation with a friendly couple who told him that Winnipeg was the "wild, wild West of Canada."

That was enough for Arnold. The Marconi Company of Windsor would wait for him in vain.

His Jewish grandparents had been farmers in Hungary. He was, at heart, a country boy who loved horses and cowboy stories and Westerns, especially John Wayne. And he'd always wanted to wear one of those tall hats.

The wildness of Winnipeg was an illusion, as he discovered all too soon.

But then, illusion, that treacherous landscape between appearances and reality, has been the landscape of Arnold Frieman's life.

Even now, at 77 years of age, it's his constant companion.

He has earned, built or acquired many worthwhile things he could only hope for: a stainless reputation in business, a beautiful home. More important, he enjoys a happy marriage, two healthy grown children, and he lives within walking distance of his five grandchildren.

It looks like the peaceful life of a very privileged man, and Arnold Frieman is grateful. He's more than willing to discuss what looks to many as his sheer good fortune.

His story is the classic rags to riches, after all.

He really did arrive in Canada with nothing in his pocket: a vagabond, in his words; no family, no friends, no English.

He brought with him also a shrapnel scar on his right shoulder, but he never mentions that.

As a war orphan, he'd ended up in Norway where he worked in Oslo as an electronic apprentice with the Marconi Company, but he was weary of war-torn Europe and desperate to leave it behind him. The outbreak of the Korean war provided the opportunity. Canada was in short supply of electronic workers, and Arnold was granted a visa, he says, "in the blink of an eye."

The Jewish Congress came to his rescue on his arrival in Winnipeg. They found him a room and board and a job paying a "respectable" $28 a week.

With the encouragement of a local Jewish couple who were particularly kind to him, Sam and Minnie Heft, Arnold decided to get himself an education. He enrolled in the University of Manitoba's Bachelor of Arts program with a double major in psychology and political science.

He remembers debating the possibility again and again. It would cost him $250 a year, an amount he considered serious money.

He was a resourceful young man accustomed to looking after himself, and he came up with a workable plan. He would use his summers to earn his tuition, driving around the U.S. in his 52 Chevy, collecting damaged car radios out of wrecked autos and bringing them back to Winnipeg for repair. Then he'd sell them, reconditioned, to radio stores across Western Canada.

When classes started, just like the rags-to-riches story, he drove a taxi (it was called Moore's then) till four in the morning and managed, most days, to show up for classes at nine.

Even romance went according to script.

In his graduating year, Arnold Frieman moderated a university panel about the future of Israel and a very pretty girl in the audience, Myra Thompson, objected loudly to some of his views. As he remembers it, she was just a kid, and he was mature man of 30, but he condescended to discuss their differences after the meeting when he gave her a lift home.

By the time he dropped her off, he was in love.

Myra's family did not return the favour, however. They were sure their daughter could do much better than Arnold Frieman, a refugee with no family, no roots, no property and, well, what kind of future, a man like that?

When he went to pick her up for an evening, even the family dog, Dixie, attacked him.

But, still according to script, true love prevailed. Arnold and Myra were married, and Arnold settled down to a management job befitting the holder of a fresh Bachelor of Arts degree.

When he grew restless and unhappy in his work, it was Myra, although she was expecting their first child, who bravely suggested he take the risk of going into business for himself.

And there happened to be a business available!

Sam Gillman had been running a TV repair shop under the Morocco night club on Portage Avenue forever, and it was time to retire. Arnold and Myra blew their savings account, all $5000 of it, on the purchase of Advance Television.

Arnold knew he wasn't a natural born salesman, but he soon discovered a definite talent for innovation.

By now he understood that Winnipeg was a thrifty town, and to compete with bigger businesses, he advertised a few TV sets at a loss (a big one; some went for a profit margin of just $10) which made him one of the city's first electronic discounters.

By 1967, Advance (with the help of a back-breaking loan of a quarter of a million dollars from the Manitoba Development Fund) had relocated to its now popular location on Portage Avenue and the business was eight times bigger than its previous store at Sergeant and McGee.

He would continue to build a reputation for leading edge ideas as the business grew; He had no clue then that electronics would explode in the coming decades, but he did have one great idea: one stop shopping for home and auto entertainment needs.

Advance got a head start in the cell phone business by partnering with MTS mobility in 1988. The company was also early off the mark when construction companies decided to build "smart homes" pre-wired for home electronics.

Arnold's electronics expertise was somewhat limited back then; he has joked that "It's a business that can fry you!" But from the start he insisted on hiring people who knew everything there was to be known, and combined that practice with the old-fashioned idea that the customer comes first. No exceptions.

A contented staff was also essential. Advance Electronics has never opened on Sundays so employees, especially people with family responsibilities, could enjoy a break. The company employs about 180 people in 2005.

Advance Pro, the commercial division of the business, secured large and lucrative corporate contracts with the company's reputation for sophistication and customer support.

Advance provided security and surveillance systems for the

Winnipeg Arena, the Convention Centre, and for Heading-ley Jail. The company also built the complex sound system for Rainbow Stage and the video system for the Manitoba School for the Deaf.

When the province of Manitoba launched their distance education project, they gave Advance Pro the job of creating a facility that would allow students in rural Manitoba to participate interactively in educational events in Winnipeg. The brand new Red River College also called on Advance's long experience to design and install a state-of-the-art electronics system and broadcast studio in its Princess Avenue building.

And the company equipped Winnipeg's MTS Centre top to bottom, with a superb quality sound system and a studio which can broadcast events live anywhere in the world. The brand new Red River College also called on Advance's long experience to design and install a state-of-the-art electronics system and broadcast studio in its Princess Avenue building.

As Advance Electronics approached its fiftieth anniversary, honours began to pour in. In 1995, the august Retail Council of Canada endowed Advance with their much coveted national Retail Excellence Award.

In 2002, Manitoba Business Magazine named Arnold Frieman Entrepreneur of the Year. He appeared, tuxedoed and smiling broadly on its cover.

And no wonder; Advance continues to prosper in a city well known for its wholesale mentality, even in an era characterized by the invasion of "big box" retailers and warehouse stores.

More than one business writer has concluded that the continuing success of Advance Electronics is unmatched in Canada.

The same can be said about the man who engineered it all, the one who still comes in every day, brings the lunch packed by his wife, and eats it at his desk.

The man with the shrapnel scar on his shoulder.

Before he turned 21 and came to Canada, the madness

of war had taught Arnold Frieman more than he wanted or needed to know about survival. Before he turned 21, he had faced risk, danger, and a fundamental aloneness that would indeed make the most cutthroat business on earth look like the proverbial picnic.

His personal war began in 1944, when Arnold was 15 and studying in Budapest.

"There were 350,000 Jews there, none of us prepared for what was coming."

When the Germans invaded in 1944 Arnold learned that in his hometown, the entire Jewish community, including his family, were being readied for shipment to Auschwitz. He managed to buy false identification papers and, in spite of the risk of being captured or killed himself, rushed home hoping to save them,

"I was too late. They were already in a cattle car on their way to the death camp."

He was devastated.

He was soon be put to work as a slave labourer in a brewery, then moved to the Russian front in Romania. In the Romanian work camp, because of his age and small size, he was made water boy. He eventually fled the custody of Romanian soldiers only to be recaptured and held prisoner in an old movie theatre with about 100 other young Jews.

He still recalls the frequent beatings, starvation, and the ever present feeling of impending death that marked those times.

Believing they would be shipped to the Russian front as prisoners of war, Arnold and the others escaped, all the while expecting to be shot on sight.

Back in his hometown in Hungary he had joined a cadre of anti-Russian youth, and soon he heard the police were looking for him, and fled to Vienna where other Jews helped him to the American Zone. He finally found himself in a displaced persons camp in Bergen Belsen.

In June of 1948, Arnold and other Jewish war orphans

were re-settled in Norway and he was given a chance to study two-way communications and apprenticed to the Norwegian Marconi Company.

But Arnold's war wasn't over.

When the Arab-Israeli conflict broke out that year, he was nineteen.

"It seemed to me that the Jews who had survived Hitler's death camps were facing the prospect of a second Holocaust. Everything would be lost, their suffering for nothing, if the state of Israel was wiped out. I couldn't do much, but I had to do what I could."

He volunteered to fight for Israel and joined a group to be trained in the basics of combat in Norway. He could work a two way radio He could clean his gun blindfolded. He learned the uses of the bayonet. He was ready to kill or be killed.

At one point the "mahalnik" (overseas volunteer) found himself part of a team in charge of 400 North African Jewish refugees on a ship headed for Israel. For 32 days they travelled from Marseilles to Haifa with failing power, the fear of sinking, little food and water, and a cacophony of languages. "To this day, I can't believe we made it." he recalls.

As a volunteer, Arnold Frieman was sent to an Israeli air force base and assigned to man the base's ground-to-air radio transmitting station He completed his tour of duty in October of 1949 and returned to Norway.

And still his war wasn't over.

"My mind set was anything but normal, sensible, or logical. I accepted whatever help came my way, but I was a young man destroyed inside, looking for a reason for living. I was disabled in the deepest sense of the word, crippled by the force of the inexplicable hatred for the Jews, and by the betrayal of the God who had refused to intervene.

I rejected the God of the Jews, if there was one. I could not get the image of the Nazi gas showers out of my mind. In the middle of the night, in the darkness, I could hear my mother screaming and imagine her watching my little sister, who was eight, and my two younger brothers choke to death in front of her.

When I went to Israel, I was looking for that God who had allowed the holocaust to happen, or at least an explanation from someone who might understand something I didn't. I looked everywhere, I went to the rabbis, I went to the chaplains in the Air Force, God was not there.

And I hated weakness, I hated the weakness of the victims, I hated the part of myself that was Jewish and therefore must be weak. I learned what it meant to hate your very self.

I was homeless to my soul.

You could say I ceased to be Jewish, but I was left with a gaping problem still, which was, what shall I be? Who shall I be?"

That was the Arnold Frieman who arrived in Canada in 1951.

In the six years which preceded his departure, he had been consumed by hatred and bereft of his family, his humanity, his identity and his hope.

He would recover them all, through the grace of another family who refused to let him slip away into bitter emptiness that threatened him.

"Minnie Heft was a soft spoken, cultured woman, unbelievably sensitive, who, along with her husband Sam, drew me back into the Jewish fold. They insisted I go with them to the synagogue. I respected them so much, (I called them Mom and Dad) that I had to go.

I started to attend synagogue on Saturdays. It was Rabbi Berkal who grabbed me; I heard him pray with such deep emotion, and I heard the prayers I had known and loved from childhood. It hit my heart so hard, my resistance seemed to dissolve imperceptibly beneath me. Eventually, my raging anti-Jewish fever left me."

Throughout his career, the re-born Arnold Frieman would, in fact, become known as a steadfast benefactor of the Jewish community, and to many other communities that needed his support.

He confesses to being a man who can't say no, and his wife Myra confirms it.

He has served on the boards of numerous institutions, and put his passion for music to particularly good use. Among his beneficiaries are the Manitoba Conservatory of Music and the Winnipeg Symphony Orchestra where he served two terms as Vice President in charge of programming.

In 1977 he collaborated with then Maestro Piero Gamba to commemorate the one hundred and fiftieth anniversary of the death of Ludwig Van Beethoven in a performance of his major works. When the Royal Winnipeg Ballet needed a portable sound system the ballet could not afford, Arnold negotiated a special price with its California maker and surrendered his own profit as well.

He's also served on the Board of Directors of Manitoba's Community Economic Development Fund and the Jewish Community Council, the Rosh Pina Synagogue and the Winnipeg Better Business Bureau. He's also served as president of Winnipeg's Joseph Wolinsky Collegiate.

He's an enthusiastic member of the board of directors of Deer Lodge Hospital and of the Dean's Advisory Council of the Faculty of Medicine, University of Manitoba.

And still, Arnold Frieman's internal war is not over.

"I reconciled with my Jewish community, but that has nothing to do with God," he explains.

In fact, he is frightened by the thought that God may not have fashioned human beings in his own image.

Quite the contrary; the countless senseless slaughters of history in the name of God suggest that men may have fashioned God in theirs.

"I'm still looking for answers, especially to this question: what was God's purpose for the Holocaust?

I guess I'm like Jacob, still wrestling with the angel."

Despite the emotional and intellectual burden that has been

his life's persistent companion, Arnold Frieman has kept his sense of humour; he's always available to share a funny story, to kibitz, to filter every day woes and worries through a good laugh. He still experiences great joy and release through listening to music, especially the Winnipeg Symphony, through being with close friends and through spending time with immediate family, his grandchildren in particular.

"At times like these, I honestly don't feel much older than I did thirty years ago."

Dr. June James

For June Marion James, it all comes down to grandmother.

Growing up in the forties and fifties in Port of Spain, Trinidad, her family home was typical of the Caribbean, busy and vibrant with neighbourhood events, extended family and friends.

But at the heart of it all was Granny.

The James household was often full of students who came to see June's father, Carlston James, a dedicated teacher, for extra help.

Sometimes he tutored them for scholarships to junior or senior high school.

Other times, when he was principal of the Young Offenders Detention Institute, they came for help in finding jobs. He never turned anyone away.

It was not unusual for young June to find the kitchen replete with thank-you gifts such as home grown vegetables or chickens.

But when someone in the family (or in the neighbourhood, for that matter) had a really pressing problem, they took it straight to Granny.

June's grandmother was not only gentle and wise. She was shrewd, clever, and a long life had made her very, very strong.

The family home had two living rooms, and the second one was an informal office. That's where Grandma ran her business. In an era well before feminism, she was a successful entrepreneur, a mortgage broker with a reputation for finding a home for anyone who really wanted one.

When powerful Granny told seven year old June that she could do anything she wanted to do, June believed her.

And Granny wanted a doctor in the family.

She would get her wish, and then some.

The little girl who had sat on her lap and hung on her every word would go away to school, would be a doctor, a medical innovator, a compassionate teacher and a community builder. Her very presence in her community would inspire young people, and help to put a roof over the heads of many who needed one.

In her new home, Canada, she would be heaped with more honours than she had time to count.

You can read about her in Who's Who in Canada, Who's Who in International Women; Canada at its Millennium; Who's Who in Black Canada, or in The Black Experience in Manitoba, a collection of memories lovingly put together by high school students in Winnipeg.

And if you suggested to Dr. June James that she had grown into the grandmother she left long ago in Port of Spain, she might tell you that was her finest achievement.

In 1960, June James was one of a very small group of Trinidadian students accepted into the University of Manitoba's Faculty of Science.

In those days, the children of educated Caribbean families often by -passed the University of the West Indies for post secondary institutions in England, but June, always an astute researcher, had done her homework.

"I hated cold weather, and I knew that in England, I'd be cold whether I was inside a house or outside of it. I figured that in Canada, I'd at least be warm inside."

There were few West Indians in Manitoba then, (a couple of hundred compared to the thriving community of 30,000 now) and June suffered not just from the bitter cold, but from homesickness.

Going home, however, was out of the question.

"For one thing, I was determined to get into medical school. For another, if I showed my face back in Trinidad, my father, who had worked hard all of his life to pay for my education, would crucify me!"

After three years of hitting the books, and hitting them hard, June applied to be admitted to the University's Faculty of Medicine.

She was accepted.

"It meant a lot, not just because it was my grandmother's fervent wish, but because an uncle of mine in Trinidad had begun medical training and had died of Typhoid Fever before he was able to graduate. So in a way, I was going to finish what someone in the family had started."

June wasn't aware until later that her admission to the University of Manitoba's faculty of medicine was a historic achievement; she was the first black woman to get in.

"I'd had the usual racist experiences…you know, apartments that were mysteriously rented when I went to see them, a certain chill in the air from a few people I had to work with, but really, there was so much work to do, I never thought about whether I was black, white or green. I just had to move ahead.

"In any case," she laughs, I was born lacking the inferiority gene."

When she graduated from medicine in 1967, the new doctor wanted to be a paediatrician, and thought early about branching into a specialty. Haematology looked good to her, but in 1970 when she a fellow in haemotology at Winnipeg's Children's Hospital, three teenagers came in closely together, all with cancer.

"It disturbed me deeply. I could tell from my reaction that I couldn't take the heartbreak of being around dying children."

That was about the time the allergy protein was discovered at John Hopkins University and in Sweden; there was terrific excitement about it. I was planning on moving to McGill University in Montreal to work in immunology, when suddenly, it moved from Montreal to Winnipeg.

The practise of allergy had immediate appeal.

In some clinical situations, as in hives or asthma, a lot of questions are needed to get the necessary information about the home or workplace environment.

"It would allow me to play detective, integrating symptoms and signs in order to determine what was going on for my patients. The diagnosis of allergies is about 20% physical examination and 80% asking the right questions. I thought of myself as Mrs. Colombo, except I wouldn't be wearing a crumpled raincoat, I'd be wearing a white lab coat."

Mrs. Colombo, as she called herself, developed into one of Canada's foremost allergists, famous for greeting people with "the allergic salute", a combination of a sniffle, a hearty swipe under the nostrils, and a great,warm smile.

"I can suspect a likely case of allergic rhinitis across a crowded room, because people will often be doing just that – constantly sniffling and swiping at their noses."

When she first began her practise, only about 5% of the population was known to suffer from allergies. Now the number has climbed to about 30%, the result of increased exposure to cigarette smoke, pets, carpets, chemicals and, perhaps, new foods. Asthma often appears between the ages of 3-5, and peaks around 40. It affects more women than men. If you get it later in life, you have it for life.

Eventually, June James introduced an entirely innovative approach to the management of Asthma.

Where once a diagnosis of asthma focused on what patients couldn't do, she emphasized a holistic and positive approach designed to discourage the stereotype of the handicapped victim. She also felt strongly that it was important to involve parents in the management of their children's allergies.

In 1978, with the enthusiastic support of the Manitoba Lung Association, she established the Family Asthma Program.

She called in play therapists for her young patients so she could talk to parents about various treatments and side effects. She involved pharmacists and dieticians. She wrote to paediatricians throughout the province explaining her family approach, and helped set up a 6 week program at Sergeant Park School during which an asthmatic child's potential could be reinforced for anyone involved in the child's care.

Doctors in Manitoba were supportive, and it seemed that everyone, not just here but in the US, jumped on the band wagon.

The program is still thriving in Manitoba, strongly supported by The Manitoba Lung Association, Children's Hospital, Concordia Hospital and Seven Oaks hospital. The approach has also expanded to include adults.

June's innovations were only part of her medical work. She also made her mark as assistant professor at the medical school from which she graduated; and as president of the College of Physicians and Surgeons of Manitoba.

The strength and sense of self-worth imparted long ago by her grandmother in Trinidad continued to inspire her, as did the rebirth of feminism in the sixties and seventies, which provided timely support as she moved through her career.

"I was energized by all the other women who were as eager to leap over ancient hurdles as I was. I met a lot of strong, successful women here in Manitoba: Bernice Sisler, Georgia Cordes, Beryl Jones and Inez Stevenson to name just a few.

And June James had a secret weapon. She had her partner, Ralph.

They had met as students in Winnipeg in the early sixties and both recognized immediately that they had too much in common to ignore.

Ralph was from Trinidad too, and June still thinks of him not just as a Bachelor of Science a Master of Education , a PhD in Chemistry and a scholar of English and Caribbean literature, but as a graduate of the railway.

"In those days, the students always knew they could get a job at Canadian National or Canadian Pacific Railways; those people never knew how many young men they put through university. They really should get a plaque for it."

June sensed a humour and trustworthiness in Ralph that made good marriage material. She was cautious, of course. Among other things, Grandmother had shared her views on the challenges and pitfalls of marriage.

June and Ralph were married in Winnipeg in 1966 and from the start, June considered herself the lucky one. Ralph not only believed in the equality of women, he loved to cook and his many domestic skills kept their home and two young sons, Roger and Robert, running smoothly.

Like June, Ralph had learned that individuals need strong community support to grow into their full potential, and he was generous with his time and energy to anyone who asked. He was a devoted teacher at the Winnipeg Adult Education Centre, the first elected president of the Manitoba Association of Rights and Liberties, and publisher of *Caribe* a popular magazine about Caribbean writers and their work. He was also an early and vocal champion of human rights in general.

When he died very suddenly in January of 1992, a shock and loss gripped not only June and their sons, but the entire black community. More than 2000 people attended his memorial service and they represented not only the city's Afro-Caribbean community, but every cultural group and every ethnic group in Manitoba.

"He would have been pleased to know that the Winnipeg School Board allowed teachers the time off to attend his memorial, a very rare gesture indeed." June says.

When Ralph and June James immigrated separately to Canada and its fledgling, somewhat tentative brand of multicultural policy, they had both brought with them the unique experience of practical multiculturalism as it had evolved in Trinidad.

The twin islands of Trinidad and Tobago are the most southerly in the Caribbean, claimed for Spain by the highly controversial adventurer, Christopher Columbus in 1492. Like many other islands, they belonged periodically also to England and France and the colonial masters all influenced their development, as did their indigenous people, the Arawak and Carib Indians.

Slave labour was imported into Trinidad and Tobago from Africa and India around the 17th century and indentured labourers from India at the beginning of the 20th century. Slavery continued until 1838. There are also significant Chinese, Lebanese and Portuguese communities, the heritage of early entrepreneurs who came as tailors, merchants and adventurers.

"There are simply too many different people living too closely together in Trinidad and Tobago to practise overt discrimination," June says, "though within recent decades politicians frequently try to capitalize on ethnic differences with the policy of 'apangat' or 'voting for your own race'

In T and T, as we say, it's been economics rather than skin color that determine where you are in the social hierarchy."

Throughout the seventies and eighties, June and Ralph James both watched Manitoba, and Winnipeg in particular, become a more sophisticated and cosmopolitan society, and saw also that new waves of people of colour needed more services and cultural sensitivity.

'The high point of immigration from the Caribbean was in the sixties; students came, graduated and got jobs; no problem. Another group came in the seventies after getting an education in Britain, again, good jobs were waiting for them. In the eighties, there was greater diversity in immigrants, both in origin and in prior education, and the number of available jobs had also fallen."

They knew also that these needs had to balanced against those of a large, awakening aboriginal population.

And they knew that for Manitoba to be a "progressive" place – one willing to take the best solutions to social problems and adapt them to local needs - would require a concerted effort of at least three very different forces; individual activists like themselves, an informed community; and co-operation from government, encompassing both political leaders and bureaucrats.

"The thing is, it's not enough for the guy at the top to preach cultural integration; if the person at the front desk on the main floor doesn't buy it, it won't happen." June says.

She points out that Manitoba once set a target of 5% visible minority employees in the provincial civil service. The New Democrats later revised this to 8%, but the actual number of "vizmin" employees remains curiously at 2%

When June threw her support behind Winnipeg's nascent International Centre in 1968, she learned a lot about the challenges facing refugees in Canada.

"It was up close and personal. The sheer number of problems could give me a headache, if I let it. I saw these people with no English, no life skills, no money, no confidence, to name a few; certainly none of the advantages I'd been blessed with."

She eventually became the very proactive president of the International Centre. When she led the search for a building that the centre could call home, she "toured every single warehouse in the Exchange district!" The Centre eventually settled on Edmonton Street.

Inevitably, the lessons of her work there, as well as with the Caribbean Canadian Association and the influential of the local and national Congress of Black Women combined with the business savvy inherited from her grandmother.

The Harambee Housing Co-operative was perhaps the most draining, demanding and rewarding public project of June's life in Canada.

The plan of the Board of Directors was to provide safe, pleasant and affordable housing for growing numbers of people who would otherwise have no access to it.

"The various housing authorities and politicians told us we were trying to build a Cadillac with a Chevy budget" June remembers. It took more than five years of dealing with tight-fisted funders and with people who didn't think it could or should be done, but, with support from the CMHC and Manitoba Housing, the 56 unit complex finally went up near the junction of Bishop Grandin and Pembina Highways.

Harambee (a Swahili word for Let's All Pull Together) still provides very desirable homes for Manitobans who've immigrated from many corners of the earth, families from Nicaragua, Russia, the Middle East, the Caribbean and Africa.

The recreation centre at Harambee is named for Ralph James.

For that work, and for her contributions to the work of the Canadian Automobile Association of Manitoba, the United Way, the Congress of Black Women, Manitoba chapter, and more recently the Winnipeg Foundation, as well as for her help in establishing better working for domestics in Manitoba, and for working towards high quality daycare to Winnipeg, June James continues to collect accolades and honours; the Governor General's 125th Anniversary medal; the YWCA's Woman of the Year Award, not to mention the Manitoba Medical Association's citation as Physician of the Year (2000) to name a few.

"Being named Physician of the Year was a total shock! They did it entirely behind my back. I was pleasantly astounded!" she comments.

In May 2004 June received The Order of Manitoba the province's highest award and In June 2004 addressed the students at Red River College convocation in Applied sciences and Aboriginal Studies as she received the alumunus award. an..Honorary Diploma. She was diligent in getting phrases both from Cree and Ojibway languages to incorporate in her speech.

She has now lived for 45 years in Manitoba, 35 of them in the service of medicine. She's still in love with her practise as an allergy and asthma specialist at the Winnipeg Clinic where she former chairman of the board and still a member of the ethics committee.

Dr. James mentors young women whenever she gets the chance and encourages them to pursue their education, especially in the sciences.

"After all these years, I'm sorry to say it's still a hard sell. We have a lot more work to do in this respect.

She tells young women that of all the skills they will need in any career they choose, the ability to chat will be crucial to their success.

"That's my trade secret," she confides. "It took me a long time to become an active listener, to wait to hear the end of someone else's sentence before speaking myself. I know now that can dramatically shorten the time it takes to solve any problem."

She muses on one particular twist of fate for her and her late husband Ralph.

"We might have gone back to the West Indies, you know.

Very early on, Ralph thought about it from time to time. When he went back to Trinidad to investigate employment opportunities, he was told he was overqualified for anything that was available. A couple of years later, still thinking of home, he applied to develop the science curriculum for the Caribbean. He never heard from them. Not a word.

In the Caribbean, in those days, anyone from abroad was considered a threat. I hope that much has changed."

"My life is not all work. I find time for gardening and golfing (thanks to Shirley and Len Layne I have new clubs and a new swing!) and travelling, and of course socializing.

"In any case, Canada became our home and it will always be home for me, my sons, my daughter in law Megan and my grandson Alexander.

Leo Mol

. . . .

Tom Lamb has been known to stop traffic on busy St. Mary's Road in south east Winnipeg.

People gawk at him from their cars; cyclists pedal up within inches to inspect his parka. Parents park their strollers and pose next to him with their babies.

Nothing distracts the famous bush pilot from his task. He continues to throw his massive strength into the propeller of what must be a small pioneer airplane, one which is invisible to everyone but him.

The power, the suffering, the vision of his life is all there on Tom Lamb's bronze face and onlookers understand it in an instant. Many are moved to think about the history of Manitoba and the awesome struggle to open up the north, some for the first time in their lives.

The monument is the creative genius, perhaps the signature piece, of Winnipeg's Leo Mol, internationally acclaimed artist and sculptor.

Art dealer David Loch is accustomed to the fuss. The bronze sculpture of Tom Lamb stands in front of his gallery and is part of his private collection.

"It's electric, it creates automatic excitement, it's everything art should be," says Loch.

Now in his nineties, Leo Mol and his wife of 61 years, Margareth live just a few blocks away in the aging Norwood house they have lived in since 1954.

Mol's studio is in the basement. From it he has produced beauty and joy in works that can be found around the world; in London, in Rome, in Vienna, in Washington. His work is so well known, so well recognized in the world of art, there's no need to sign it. It speaks for itself.

The man who has sculpted popes, prime ministers and presidents has been invited many times to move to more exciting places than the smallish isolated city he chose to make his home. He has always declined to leave.

David Loch, his long time friend and agent, knows why.

"He came here in search of freedom, and he found it. Money and material things mean nothing to him. He lives to work, to move people in the way his portrait of Tom Lamb moves people. That is the meaning of his life. He has been safe here. There was never a need to move anywhere else."

Leo Mol certainly was not born into freedom and safety.

He was born Leonid Molodoshanin in 1915 in Polonne, near Shepetivka, Ukraine, into a family of potters who, like most of their neighbours, made their subsistence living working with the rich local clay.

His father Georgi and mother Olga were loving parents who had high hopes for their son, a lad who loved to play with and shape the clay under his feet almost as soon as he could speak.

When the boy showed an interest in drawing, his father encouraged it, even spending too much money on a book for him about the history of art, a generosity he was later to regret.

"My father wanted me to follow in his footsteps, but I had discovered Michelangelo, and I wanted to be an artist." Leo remembers.

"He told me every housewife needs a pot to cook – she doesn't need a painting. Being an artist was not his idea of a worthy life."

But having got passionately interested in the history of art, Leo was determined to go to Austria to study painting, and after many long and bitter arguments, his parents relented. When their son turned fifteen, they reluctantly put him on the train to Vienna, where he arrived with almost no money, but a willingness to take any job or do any work that would support him.

His awe and appreciation for the architecture, the ancient squares and monuments of the beautiful city expressed itself in sketches which, to his great surprise, passers by were willing to pay for. Soon he was enrolled at a small night class for would-be artists where the teacher examined his paintings and told him "You paint like a sculptor."

"She was right. And that's when I knew what I wanted to do."

Leo Mol spent several happy years in Vienna until an influential teacher there directed him to Germany, where some of the finest and best known European sculptors were working and teaching..

He took that advice and somewhat tentatively, still unsure of himself, applied to the Berlin Academy. He was accepted. At the same time, he experienced the heady success of selling more and more drawings and works in terra cotta.

His peaceful and moderately prosperous life in Berlin was shattered by the outbreak of the Second World War. As a Slav trapped in Germany, he was in special danger. People were rounded up and sent to camps in almost random way, and his anxiety for the safety of his family in the Ukraine and for his own in Berlin grew steadily.

But he had fallen in love; he and Margareth met in 1942 and married the following year.

He remembers a conversation that put everything in perspective for him.

"One day one of my colleagues pointed to a tall street lamp.

'See that pole?' he said. 'When the Russians get here, you'll be swinging from it!'"

In the spring of 1945, the Russians were indeed closing in on Berlin, and Leo and Margareth fled the city, two small drops in a river of refugees rushing to the West. He would learn later that his father and his brother, also a promising artist, both died in a Siberian work camp.

"Margareth and I were lucky to find room in a train to Amsterdam."

Very lucky, it turned out, because the refugee camp which became their temporary home was near a small ceramic factory where Leo found work making moulds for the figurines they sold. The work lasted till the factory burned down about a year later.

But even the fire brought good luck. Out of work, Leo decided to start his own business, albeit a small one run mostly on credit, and, ironically, soon he became the successful potter his father had always hoped for.

The couple loved the life in Holland. It was sophisticated and congenial, open minded with lots of amateur artists whose company they enjoyed immensely. Leo began to attract and accept commissions and started attending classes at the noted Hague Academy.

It was here that Leo Molodoshanin decided he would be known as Leo Mol; a much shorter, more manageable name to sign to his work.

Looking back, Leo concluded that their four years in Holland were some of the happiest they had ever known.

"It was a period of light, both spiritually and physically" Leo told art critic Paul Duval many years later. "If it had not been for the infamous Berlin Blockade of 1948 by the Russians and our fear of being trapped again by war, it is possible we might have stayed there."

He had long been interested in the history and culture of Argentina; that was a possible new home for the young artist and his wife. But Margareth spoke excellent English, and they had friends in western Canada, where they heard that many Ukrainians had settled well.

When he visited the offices of the Canadian immigration department in The Hague, the interviewer there reminded Leo of his father.

"He asked me what I did to earn a living and of course I said I am an artist, a sculptor. He was not impressed. He said the country didn't need sculptors, it needed farmers! I told him I knew lots of farmers there, though.

I'm glad he didn't ask me who they were, and I promised to work for them.

He wasn't too happy, but he gave us the visas we needed."

Much to the disappointment of their many Dutch friends, Leo and Margareth left Holland for Canada in December of 1948.

"Margareth cried for two years," Leo said.

The tears were not just for homesickness, for their former life in Holland. They arrived at their friend's farm near Prince Albert, Saskatchewan on the uncommonly frigid New Years Eve of 1949.

"At first we couldn't see the people for all their winter clothes. Later we couldn't see them at all behind the tall snow banks."

People in their new community re-assured them that spring would come, but for the newcomers, time seemed to stand still. There was nothing to do in winter, and Leo was soon looking for the nearest big city.

It was Winnipeg.

He caught the train and stepped off of it knowing nobody and speaking no English, but the sight of a church supply store made him feel at home. The owner was Ukrainian, and when he heard Leo was also Ukrainian, and an artist, he promptly hired him for twenty dollars a week. He would do whatever artistic work the church needed; icons, perhaps some carving, some decoration.

Leo Mol was overjoyed; a working artist again, and in Canada!

Not long after that, Margaret joined him from Saskatchewan, and once she became a qualified teacher at the Winnipeg Normal school, got a job in a country school near Beausejour.

By 1952, the couple were living comfortably in a small downtown apartment in Winnipeg, and Leo had found a suitable studio for reasonable rent.

His extensive travelling and his carefully honed skills of observation suggested to him that surprisingly few artists were offering collectible art with Canadian themes. He would do that.

No one was interested in locally made art with Canadian subjects like square dancers and Eskimo hunters, but a buyer at Birk's jewellers agreed to take a look at Leo's work and liked what he saw. Today, art collectors count those early Winnipeg ceramics among the most desirable ever created in Canada.

Leo and Margareth settled into the house in Norwood in 1956, and Leo's interest in competitions and commissions continued to grow. One of his biggest disappointments came when he placed second in the Manitoba contest to design a monument to the brilliant Ukrainian poet and nationalist Taras Shevchenko, a man for whom he felt the deepest admiration.

Oddly enough, a competition Leo Mol entered in 1963 but did not win was to prove a turning point in his life and in his career.

A Winnipeg church had awarded a commission for a

stained glass window to a Ukrainian American artist named Sviatoslav Hordynsky.

Though he was a well respected translator, the artist could neither hear nor speak. When he requested that the church hire a local assistant, they provided him with Leo Mol.

Asked to look at Hordynsky's design, Leo showed Hardynsky his own idea. Hardynsky not only insisted that the church use Leo's window instead of his own, he urged Leo to enter more aggressively into international design contests. He encouraged him specifically to enter a worldwide competition for a monument to Taras Shevchenko to be erected by a large and influential Ukrainian American population in Washington DC.

His success in that competition introduced Leo Mol to the world spotlight.

The job meant spending two years working in a studio in Staten Island, New York, time he spent renewing his understanding and appreciation of Shevshenko, experimenting with every detail which might communicate the man's greatness as a poet, painter and leader. It also provided him with the opportunity to do plentiful sketches of the live models at New York's art schools, many of which later became bronzes.

The unveiling of the Shevchenko monument was attended by over a hundred thousand people. Former President Dwight Eisenhower arrived by helicopter to unveil it. It was a cover story on Newsweek Magazine!

At the unveiling, an aide to Eisenhower asked Leo if he'd consider sculpting a bust of the former president and war hero, a project that appealed to him deeply. In the two weeks that the artist and his subject spent together at Eisenhower's Gettysburg home, they compared experiences in the war and their mutual interest in art. In the family's kitchen, Eisenhower was an eager student of the sculpting process and Leo his willing teacher.

On the 25th anniversary of the unveiling of the Shevchenko monument, Leo returned to Washington and stole a few moments to wander through the city's National Portrait Gallery. He was moved to ask why there was no exhibition devoted to Eisenhower, and learning that the Gallery had nothing to exhibit, offered them all of his own memorabilia, which they gratefully accepted.

"That was typical of Leo," David Loch comments. "It never occurred to him what his work cost him – the materials, the travel, the time. He's an uncommonly generous man."

Loch believes that because Leo Mol lived and worked in Winnipeg – a small, unassuming city of modest means – many unusual things were possible.

"He bought a house just six years after arriving in Canada. He was a classic workaholic producing a huge volume of work at relatively low costs. His clients never overpaid for his paintings, drawings or bronzes. In fact he probably never charged a correct price for anything he created, and it was a huge bonus that he actually kept one of most of the work he produced."

It was the artist's personal methods and habits, combined with his generosity and love for his home in Winnipeg that would help give the city one of its foremost attractions, the Leo Mol Sculpture Garden.

Its very existence is a stunning achievement, given that, when Leo arrived in Manitoba "There was no sense of sculpture here, other than the cry of shock at the sight of a naked woman. Now, almost every child knows how to look at sculpture."

Although the dream of a collection of superb statuary in a unique park setting probably occurred to many of Mol's admirers, it was his friend and agent David Loch who brought it to life.

"Here was this unrivalled body of work that needed a permanent home, something other than a conventional institution where it might end up in pristine, unlit vaults, from which it might or might not emerge for occasional public enjoyment. And here was this sprawling green space known as Assiniboine Park which had an untended stretch of bush surrounding a gardener's house in dilapidated condition...and here was this artist willing to donate his life work to the city that welcomed him..."

It was an intoxicating idea, and we had all the expertise we needed to see it through."

The Leo Mol Garden was especially significant because it kept the artist's body of work together.

"As far as bronze portraiture goes, no one can touch Leo Mol." says David Loch, "and Leo's work is unique because in part because it brings together his formal, "old school" European training and the unexpected subject matter he found in Canada, original characters like Tom Lamb, and of course, the animals he so loved to sculpt. But no matter how great an artist's work may be, if it gets split up, it can disappear from sight and be forgotten."

With the co-operation of then mayor Bill Norrie, the fundraising influence and civic leadership of Hartley Richardson, a solid board of volunteers in place, the cautious promise of a million dollars from city council and David Loch's own personal line of credit on the line, the work began.

Gary Hilderman and Associates provided the breathtaking landscape.

Leo Mol walked through the space and walked through it again. He placed every sculpture himself. There are more than two hundred of them.

"The first time I saw the first phase completed, I stood and cried like a baby' says David Loch. "The almost translucent little gallery, the pool...the grace of the arrangements... I knew how it would look, but I wasn't prepared for how it would feel!

You could feel that the sight of it would beckon and entertain people for the rest of time!"

In the second phase, Leo Mol's former studio, the one room country school house in which he had worked for many years, was moved into the garden as well. Inside, visitors can see portraits in process; Moses, Queen Elizabeth, the Pope.

In winter Leo Mol's sculpture garden is blanketed in snow, but every summer about a quarter of a million people wander through its paths. Doctors are known to send their patients there to relax and de-stress; families come with out of town guests; some people come to meditate or to practise tai chi among the sculptures at dawn.

Leo Mol comes too. He takes a city bus to the park (he can no longer drive a car) and his mind sometimes drifts between the past and the present, but he likes to wander the paths and talk to people looking at his work.

"Not too much blah blah, though. It should speak for itself" he says

Sometimes, unseen and unrecognized, he naps on one of the benches.

His wife Margareth says the sculpture garden means everything to him, more than the highest honours his contemporaries have given him.

She teases him: 'My garden, my garden' you tell me. It's not yours! You gave it to the people!"

So he did.

And he insisted that admission be free, so everyone could enjoy it.

Dr. Rey Pagtakhan

. . . .

Three things can be said of Reynaldo D. Pagtakhan that can be said of very few others.

He once almost disappeared in snow.

He chose to immigrate to Canada not once, but twice.

And he's proof that a person elected to high office can be trusted to accomplish significant things for those who elected him.

Canadians would have no difficulty believing the misadventure in snow and would certainly be willing to believe someone might choose to live in Canada more than once.

It's that third claim that defies belief.

According to a poll conducted by the Trudeau Foundation in 2005, only one in four Canadian citizens trusts "the government" to do what is right. And almost 60% believe "the government" doesn't care what ordinary people think.

The same poll suggests that Canadians, like people everywhere, are voting in fewer and fewer numbers because they are certain that politicians forget about them once they're in office.

But then, most Canadians haven't paid much attention to Citizen Pagtakhan.

He's a Doctor of Medicine, Master of Science in Perinatal Physiology, Doctor of Laws, former Professor of Paediatrics and Child Health, four-term Member of Parliament (MP), former Parliamentary Secretary to the Prime Minister of Canada, and former Minister of more important things than any one person can truthfully remember. He is now Director of the newly established Global College at the University of Winnipeg which is dedicated to research, dialogue and action around global citizenship.

Even so, he's never asked for much attention.

On the contrary, he is frequently so quiet in meetings that even in full public spotlight, he can slip right under the radar.

This is partly because it's an effort for him to subvert his natural humility. It's also his birthright as a Filipino.

"I learned growing up that it's important to show humility in success, that you respect authority, that you wait until you are recognized before you speak. I'm old school generation. I tend to be silent till the time is right."

It would be a mistake, however, to conclude that Rey Pagtakhan's noticeable reticence is an indication that he has nothing to say.

His record, as we will see, shows that he is unafraid to say whatever he thinks necessary, and further, to act on it.

****

The first Filipino to be elected to high office in North America grew up in a culture which believed, before it was fashionable, that "it takes a village to raise a child."

Rey Pagtakhan was born in a missionary hospital in Tondo, Manila in 1935, and grew up in the village of Bacoor in the province of Cavite, about 17 kilometres south of that city. His mother was a teacher and his father a self-taught accountant, and he was the sixth of eleven children.

Wages were desperately low, so his mother bought and sold used goods from their home and his dad also drove a "Jeepney" van which served as a local taxi for eight to ten passengers at a time. All of Rey's brothers and sisters were self - supporting students. The family would eventually have a business woman, a dentist, two lawyers, an engineer, a physician, three accountants, a sales person, and a baker. His Nanay and Tatay (mom and dad) were selected Parents of the Year in their town.

Rey's first job, selling bread for the local bakery, started in grade school and would continue until he was almost ready to practise medicine.

The community found it hard to support schools for its children, and Rey's education might have ended in grade six, but that a private secondary school opened in his town just as he needed it.

"I remember once winning an award for high marks, but I could not accept it because I had no shoes to wear. Instead I hid behind a hedge, and after they announced my name, I went home. I didn't think this should happen to anyone. I started thinking then about how to help change things for the poor."

His secondary school was run by a Presbyterian Minister, but two years later, when education authorities learned that the headmaster hadn't been collecting fees from his students, they shut it down. Rey, a keen if not well to do student, was able to transfer to another school in the nearby city of Pasay.

In high school, he was an advocate for his classmates, class president, and dreaming many professional dreams, none of which he or his parents could afford. He thought about working his way through school to a future as a lawyer or journalist, but, despite their modest means, his parents wanted him to be a doctor.

"When we get sick, we get poorer" they would say. When Rey won a place in pre-med studies, a wealthy neighbour gave him an interest-free loan to cover his tuition. Older sisters and brothers, and other relatives also helped to pay for his studies.

Going to university meant a three-hour round trip trek every day and by the end of his first semester, the young student was worn out. Unknown to him, a classmate told her professor about Rey's awkward circumstances. Hoping to encourage the young man to finish his education, the benevolent professor offered Rey the use of his cottage on campus. In return, Rey tutored the professor's younger son and daughter in math, algebra and physics.

"That's how things got done in a community that lacked the most basic resources," Rey recalls.

Thanks to an unending series of similarly kind sponsors - classmates and professors – Rey Pagtakhan managed to finish medical school in 1961.

He remembers every step of the struggle.

He wanted to but did not pursue his residency at the University of the Philippines General Hospital in Manila, because the sum of eight pesos (about three dollars) a month would not allow him to help his younger siblings. Instead, he accepted a Research Associate position from his paediatric professor when they received a training grant from United Pharmaceuticals.

When his first research paper in paediatric epidemiology won the first prize from the Manila Medical Society, he was thrilled, especially so because one of his professors won second prize in the same competition.

The next professional choice wasn't difficult to make.

"In those days, to be honest, likely not too many in the Philippines had heard or thought about Canada. That wouldn't really change until the later sixties and early seventies when this country began recruiting garment workers and offering the family re-unification opportunities. For medical students, the place to go for credentials was the United States of America."

In 1963, Rey Pagtakhan accepted a residency in paediatrics without having to do an internship at St. Louis Children's Hospital of Washington University School of Medicine in Missouri, where two years later he would hold a two-year Research Fellowship in Paediatric Cardiology from both the Missouri and St. Louis Heart Associations

He'd met a wonderful woman during his internship in Manila. Gloria Visarra is the daughter of a very strict family who followed Filipino traditions, which meant a carefully supervised courtship. She'd completed a Bachelor of Science in Foods and Nutrition at Centro Escolar University, and, not at all coincidentally, applied to St Louis University to pursue a Master of Science in Dietetics.

They were married in a late fall wedding in Missouri in 1964.

After four and half years in the USA, the couple decided to move to Canada and chose Winnipeg so that Rey could prepare to be a specialist in lung diseases of children. At that time, there was no such specialty in the Philippines where he had hoped to practise. He chose Winnipeg when he read that a Dr. Victor Chernick, just returned from Johns Hopkins University and a Queen Elizabeth Scientist awardee, was in charge of the training program.

Their winter road trip from Missouri to Manitoba in January of 1968 introduced Rey and Gloria Pagtakhan to the secret life of snow.

His close encounter of the frozen kind happened in North Dakota, just outside Grand Forks during a coffee stop at a small gas station. Hoping to be the gallant husband, Rey decided to pull the car right over to the door from which Gloria would shortly emerge.

He couldn't know that the hard surface snow that appeared

to be solid ground was in fact, just icing on a deep ditch, and he drove the car nose down and tail up right into it.

"Through sheer luck, I escaped without injury or damage to the car, but my pride was definitely wounded."

Things didn't get much better when the Pagtakhans finally pulled into a frigid Winnipeg. The basement apartment they had rented sight unseen wasn't properly heated, so the couple decided to walk to a hotel. They found one they thought must be safe; there were police everywhere. It was the infamous and now defunct Leland, and unknown to them, stuff of many rough legends in Winnipeg.

In 1969, Rey Pagtakhan completed a Master of Science in Perinatal Physiology at the University of Manitoba.

By 1972, the couple had two small children . They felt a strong pull to be with both their families in the Philippines, although he had earlier joined the Faculty of Medicine at the University of Manitoba as lecturer and the Children's Hospital of Winnipeg as consultant in lung diseases. When his father-in-law died that year, they decided to make the long trip back for the funeral, and later investigate the possibilities of teaching and practising there.

Three days after their arrival in Manila, Ferdinand Marcos declared Martial law in the Philippines. It would last 14 years.

The young family felt privileged to return to the sanctuary of Canada. It was the second and final time they chose to live here. Rey pursued his clinical practice, teaching and research, published several papers and chapters for medical journals and textbooks, received more awards and honors, and rose to the rank of full Professor. Rey and Gloria became citizens in 1974.

"I still remember that hair-raising citizenship test. I studied and studied, I even memorized the words to O Canada, but they didn't ask me to sing it. Instead they asked me, out of ten questions, what was the biggest port in Manitoba and I was completely floored. It was Churchill, of course, but try as I might, I couldn't remember. But I managed to pass. It felt wonderful!!!"

His practice as a pediatric respiratory specialist was always a busy one. That and a growing family left little time for anything else, but other people frequently brought issues in the Filipino community to his attention.

One persistent problem was especially important to its prominent doctor, and that was a constant division over how the Filipino culture should be portrayed and communicated to other diverse cultural groups in Manitoba. Many thought that, with his leadership, the community might come together on it.

Rey Pagtakhan agreed to get involved. Three months after assuming the leadership of one Filipino association, the community was united.

Something real had been accomplished. Victory was sweet. The political bug had taken a tiny bite.

His next political forum would be in his own neighbourhood; he decided to run for the St. Vital School Board, where he tackled tough issues like quality assurance in schools and was known as "the rebel in a suit."

With his excellent reputation in medicine and in local politics well established, it was almost inevitable that Rey Pagtakhan would someday be approached to get involved with a political party.

In 1986, he had been impressed and inspired by the eloquence of federal Liberal leader John Turner, and began to think about the role politics should be playing in the solution of public problems, but he'd never thought of running for national office. He'd also spent a lot of time reading the autobiographies of Abba Eban, noted Israeli foreign minister, and Anwar el-Sadat, former president of Egypt. These suggested to him that politics was not necessarily as contemptible a vocation as popularly believed. In fact, they confirmed for him the nobility of politics.

"There were things I really cared about because of my

experiences with poverty as a child; the social value of education, poverty itself, medical care, the status of visible minorities. The question was whether anything worthwhile could be done about them through politics." he says.

In 1984, the late Senator Gil Molgat recruited him for volunteer work in the Liberal party. Four years later, he was surprised to find himself a candidate. He was elected in his first race, and would go on to hold his seat in the next three federal elections.

At least one media described his victory as "a classic immigrant success story", but Rey Pagtakan had other thoughts about it.

"That first success was an important one because it was the first time a Filipino Canadian had been elected Member of Parliament. I think it served to open the eyes of visible minority communities right across the country. More and more of their members from all political parties were running as candidates and were being elected.

Following his election in 1988, Dr. Pagtakhan took a political leave of absence from teaching and the active practice of medicine, but the two disciplines of medicine and politics were not as radically different as they appeared.

"From the very first political work I did, I could see that one could approach medical and political problems in the same way. When a patient brought me a problem, I identified the chief complaint, (the issue); I did a history and physical exam (got all the information); I did tests and lab work (collected documents); made a diagnosis, and prescribed action.

It was this practical rather than primarily partisan approach that would earn him the reputation as both an independent thinker and exemplary constituency politician.

'I loved my constituency work. I tried to see hundreds of cases through every year. For example, constituents would come to me who were not aware of the availability of the disability provision of the Canada Pension Plan and because they were late claiming it, were denied altogether.

That's ridiculous! A right that is given to you by parliament should not have a time limit! That law was amended." He says with satisfaction.

He felt even greater satisfaction when he was able to prevent the deportation of a handful of immigrants and succeeded in actually bringing back to Canada two deportees on humanitarian grounds.

In 1994, *The Toronto Star* National Affairs Columnist Carol Goar summed up the unusual media approval which has accompanied Rey Pagtakhan's career when she wrote that "in six years of parliament, he's accomplished more than most backbenchers do in an entire career. And he's done it without making deals, trading favours or indulging in political theatrics"

Both media and the public were impressed when he called for a public enquiry into Canada's blood distribution system after hundreds of patients were given HIV tainted blood; that he helped win compensation for haemophiliacs infected with the AIDS virus and convinced Liberal strategists to include a prenatal nutrition program in the party's election program.

One other issue he continues to champion is the accreditation of foreign-obtained credentials, also included in the Liberals platform.

Manitobans paid even closer attention to the childproof lighter chapter of Pagtakhan's career. In October of 1994 four teenagers were killed in a fire on Winnipeg's Home Street. Two months later an 18-month old baby boy died following another fire. In both those cases, children playing with lighters were found responsible, but the MP for Winnipeg North didn't think so.

"Those fires were preventable fires," he said publicly.

"A local doctor, Milt Tennenbein had been crusading for childproof lockers for years but not succeeding because he didn't fully know how the political process worked. I put the case before the Minister of Health, then Dianne Marleau, and by June we had new regulations banning the sale of disposable lighters without childproof locks. Those regulations are still there, still saving the lives of toddlers."

In 1996, Rey Pagtakhan was elevated to the lofty status of Parliamentary Secretary to Prime Minister Jean Chretien, though the MP had publicly taken issue with his government's immigration policy.

"I knew someone with Rey's style and pre-occupations would help me keep my feet on the ground." The Prime Minister said. It was an enormously popular choice.

In this capacity, Rey gave the PM two pieces of advice (which he is not permitted to disclose) on high profile issues. "All I can tell you is that the ideas I suggested to him were not the majority opinion. But he followed both suggestions, and both turned out to be the right ones."

The decision to name Rey Pagtakhan Minister of Veterans Affairs in 2002 was widely viewed as a signal that the federal government was ready to heal the ailing relationship between Canada's veterans and the department which was supposed to serve them.

Under his leadership, the government announced compensation for benefits previously denied to Canada's native veterans who had fought in the Second World War and Korea. It was a total package of $39 million dollars. On "compassionate grounds" First Nations veterans and their spouses would be offered up to $20,000 each.

A lesser known achievement was his determination to secure compensation for former Canadian prisoners of war who applied years after the law had been repealed. Two prisoners of war had been lobbying for this benefit, and Pagtakhan offered it to them and to seventeen other veterans in the same situation, invoking the ex-gratia principle under Ministerial discretion. He also extended survivor benefits to spouses of deceased veterans for life.

Without the representation of Rey Pagtakhan, Winnipeg

probably would not have acquired the Seven Oaks Wellness Centre, the first centre in Canada to boast acute, rehabilitative and preventive care under the same roof; might not have secured the $80 million necessary for the upgrading of the Winnipeg Floodway, or the financing for the International Centre for Infectious Diseases, which is modelled after the prototype in Atlanta, Georgia. They were all projects close to his heart.

No less close to his heart was the funding for the establishment of the new Philippine Canadian Centre of Manitoba, as well as the support for the Sikh, Muslim, Hindu, and Greek cultural centres.

"These centres provide a gathering place, a home for these communities and help them promote and preserve their cultural heritage for the benefit of all of us."

There were two other special projects that particularly attracted his personal attention. He felt the Red River community in the north end of Winnipeg had been in dire need of a new centre for a very long time. The Leila Avenue development was equally in need of urgent attention since a young boy in the neighbourhood had drowned in a neglected culvert. He'd fought for both these communities as a backbencher and as opposition member.

Rey Pagtakhan did not forget either of them when he became senior federal minister for Manitoba. At his first opportunity, he persuaded the reluctant city and provincial governments to go ahead with the projects.

"A good project in opposition should remain a good project when in government." he says

His more than fifteen years in Canada's parliament came to an end when he lost the election in 2004. About that loss he said , "Defeat can be the greatest of victories. It tests your commitment to issues that matter to people. It tests your faith in the nobility of politics, it tests your faith in the supremacy of the people. It certainly tests your humility."

He has not lost his passion and activism for people. Rather

than focusing on leisurely pastimes he now busies himself with volunteer activities in the same communities that propelled him into politics.

He gladly accepted the invitation from Dr. Lloyd Axworthy, Canada's former Minister of Foreign Affairs and now President and Vice Chancellor of the University of Winnipeg, to co-chair with him the brainstorming conference recently hosted by the New Global College on "The Role of Canadian Diaspora in Global Diplomacy and Policy-Making."

There is no shortage of tangible results to which Rey Pagtakhan can point as his legacy, but the intangible effects of his life in this country may be even more crucial to its development

Of the man who was educated as a boy by the generosity of his community, who has never forgotten his roots, then Prime Minister Jean Chretien may have made the best observation.

"Rey," he said, "represents what this country is all about."

Shahina Siddiqui

It was said that the world changed on September 11, 2001.

Later, that statement became an icon of ethnocentrism; it became clear that the world had changed most dramatically for Americans. For the first time in history, citizens of the world's richest, most powerful country understood that they too were vulnerable to attack at home from outside forces.

But for selected people, not necessarily American, the world really did change. Winnipeg's Shahina Siddiqui knows this because she is one of them.

"Ten minutes after the news reached Winnipeg that terrorists had engineered the attack on the twin towers in New York, the media was at my front door. Also at my back door, and on the telephone.

Muslim communities everywhere froze.

There were distress calls from Muslims in Washington,

New York, one of them reporting that there was a mob outside."

In the next 48 hours, Shahina Siddiqui, who came to Canada from Pakistan as the wife of an accountant, who considered herself a housewife, a mother, and a volunteer in her community became an acutely public figure.

Many people thrown into the centre of a sudden, worldwide hostility may have run, may have hidden, may have declined to accept responsibility.

But, despite moments of deepest fear and anxiety, Shahina Siddiqui took her place as spokesperson for Canadian Muslims, and for her beloved and beleaguered faith, Islam.

She was ready.

"There were times in my life when I wanted to help, but I didn't know how. But life has taught me. Now I know."

Looking back, it seems her whole life had actually prepared her for leadership.

****

Sitting in the cool green study of her Charleswood home, its walls covered with messages of thanks and appreciation and enough conference speaker badges to decorate several Christmas trees, Shahina relaxes in her shalwar kameez, the traditional pants and tunic of Pakistan, this one flowered cotton. The hajib or head scarf worn as a sign of modesty in public is put away.

Her warmth and eloquent manner of speaking give her a certain dignity in spite of a naturally casual style; always in a hurry, she's been known to show up for national television appearances in her slippers.

There are files on the desk, on bookcases, on the floor. She ignores the flashing message light on her phone. She has said her prayers and cleared her morning of the spiritual counselling she would otherwise be doing.

North American Muslims number about seven million in the US and about 700,000 in Canada. There are only a handful of counsellors to serve more than 5,000 members of Manitoba's Muslim population. Shahina has trained the others.

She's interrupted her preparations for a trip to Chicago. Muslim chaplains from American prisons and hospitals have invited her to deliver one of the courses she's designed for counsellors. She also conducts cultural and spiritual literacy workshops for service providers including police and RCMP.

In spite of a debilitating iron deficiency which occasionally makes it impossible to get out bed in the morning, Shahina will make it to Chicago, and anywhere else she feels she is needed.

The example of sacrifice and dedication was set for her by the women of her childhood, an abundance of teachers, aunties, mentors, and, above all, her mother and her grand-mothers.

"There's a reason that the prophet (Mohammed) put such a high value on mothers," she says with her quick, dimpled grin.

"He was asked three times whom Muslims should serve in order to gain God's pleasure and company in Paradise, and every time, he answered, 'Your mother!'

Shahina grew up in the Karachi home of her paternal grandmother whose name translated as Star Among Women. Her grandmother was less than five feet tall, and was mar-ried at 13 to a man more than twice her age. She bore 13 children, six of whom died at an early age. In the era of the British Raj, her grandfather owned an estate unimaginable now; it encompassed no less than eighty villages.

"Her family lost it all, but that was immaterial to her. As it turned out, her story went from riches to rags and back to riches. The multi-generational home we shared with her was comfortable and full of relatives and servants, always some-one to love you when you needed it most." Shahina recalls.

It was Shahina's mother, a home schooled woman herself, who saw to it that Shahina and her sister had every chance at a formal education.

"Her biggest regret was she didn't have the chance to go herself, so she took it upon herself to enrol us in the Roman Catholic School

It was one of the best English immersion schools in Pakistan. My mother did not speak English and wore the burka, so she took a friend to translate her wishes to the nuns. Mission accomplished, she went home and presented what she had done, which was very daring, in religiously sound terms. She won the reluctant approval of the rest of the family to send us to the Christian school.

"I tell you, I have said more than my share of Hail Mary's!"

Her mother also contributed to Shahina Siddiqui's well known respect for religions other than her own, an attitude which has helped to bring Manitobans of radically different religions and cultures closer together.

"At 15, my mother was caught in the violent mobs during the partition of India and Pakistan. She witnessed many killings, burnings, lootings and rapes, but she never spoke ill of Hindus or of Sikhs. She made sure we understood that atrocities were committed on both sides. In fact she reminded us that it was a Hindu bus driver who delivered the women of her family to safety, thereby endangering his own life."

Shahina's mother and father immigrated to Canada in 1977. Her mother continued to live here after Shahina's father, a noted journalist in Pakistan, passed away. Her mother's death in 2004 left her acutely aware of the strength of character her mother had always displayed.

The Catholic convent school to which Shahina and her sister were entrusted turned out to be a brilliant choice.

"I was slightly dyslexic and not a great speller, plus I was absent a lot from class because of my iron deficiency problems...I think I was a failing student until about grade six, but my teachers managed to see beyond my handicaps.

I remember one in particular, Sister Ann Avaria. During

one test I was so nervous, she picked me up and put me in her lap and told me how smart I was, what a wonderful girl I was...saying all the right things to a quivering rabbit! My sister was right there, of course, to tell me my answers were all wrong!"

Without those difficulties in school, she is certain she could not have become a truly compassionate counsellor herself.

Later, at the all girl St Joseph's College at the University of Karachi, Shahina's hope was to be "an amazing actress" someday. She'd done Shakespeare in school, loved Keats and Wordsworth, and her mother had taught her to appreciate the beauty of Persian poetry and literature; she had a gift for satire and visions of Broadway.

When she finally saw Broadway in 1974, however, it was not as an actress but as the cultured bride of the ambitious and sophisticated accountant with whom a marriage had been arranged by both their mothers.

She met her husband Iqbal for the first time on their wedding day.

'Our mothers were certain we were well suited to each other. They were right. We're very different in our personalities – I'm a talker, and he's a man of few words, for example–but our values around important things are the same."

Iqbal's career took them almost immediately to a home on 80th Street on the east side of Manhattan.

New York City was a big adjustment for the girl who had never been out of Pakistan, who didn't drive, who'd never been to a bank. There was no family there; few people smiled or attempted to make eye contact.

The same sister who had teased Shahina when they were at school together in Karachi had moved to Brandon, Manitoba and in 1974 invited the Sidddiquis to her daughter's second birthday party. The newly weds accepted, and, in a holiday spirit, made a side trip to Winnipeg.

"It was a beautiful spring. The streets were breathtakingly

leafy. I just felt there was a soul here."

Once an investigation had revealed that the city with soul also needed accountants; they decided to re-locate to the smaller, and hopefully more friendly city immediately. In 1979, Canada welcomed them as citizens.

Amid great joy, two sons were born; first Riaz, followed by Omar.

When he was five, Riaz was diagnosed with an incurable and inevitably fatal brain disease. Medical experts told his grieving parents that the child might live for another six months.

"He was such a happy, energetic kid; he was a joy. It was hard to believe and harder still to accept," says Shahina."

"We made him the total focus of our family life.

It was sad to see him get around in his wheelchair, and the saddest day was when he lost his ability to speak.

Riaz lived to be nine years old, long enough to leave an indelible impression on his mother, his father and his brother.

"On his death our happiness was shattered and it was tempting to ask, why me?" Shahina remembers, "but it was more important to ask, why not me? The faith teaches that whom God loves most, he tries most. I may have been a Muslim in name only until then."

It was through this suffering that Shahina realized there were no support services for Muslim families in Winnipeg, nowhere to turn for guidance and solace.

Shahina vowed to change that.

Ironically, life in Winnipeg also refined Shahina Siddiqui's understanding of her faith.

"When we first lived in an apartment, neighbours invited me over for a hot dog and a beer, but I couldn't have either one," she says. On another occasion the couple were invited to go dancing.

Somebody asked me why I was a Muslim, and if I couldn't have any "fun." I'd been reading the Koran since I was 13, but I couldn't answer these questions. I went home and cried.

Then I got serious.

I can tell you that I am a different woman now. I have submitted to the creator, and He has given me purpose, meaning and peace.

Shahina continued to study Islam and to reach out to Muslims in Winnipeg and in Manitoba. The idea of the Islamic Social Services Association started in her kitchen, and soon she had the satisfaction of seeing real issues and practical problems being confronted through the establishment of this organization in 1999.

"I was a voice in the wilderness then, but I was intent on making the Mosque a woman-friendly place, and helping new families with the difficult transition to life in a Western setting. For example, previously, in the event of domestic violence, the extended family could take care of it in the home. But here, without benefit of family, safe interventions might be needed. Those supports had to be in place."

`As she worked, she saw the Muslim community grow larger and more diverse than she could have imagined, with professionals, young families, students and refugees arriving from South Asia and Africa, as well as Bosnia and Kosovo.

She and other local Muslim leaders were keen to avoid the problems faced especially by young Muslims in Great Britain.

"If you have an influx of the young who do not feel accepted, known and respected, who lack validation of any kind, you will have rebels on your hands."

Her personal solution was to write, speak, educate and travel Manitoba and North America introducing interested people to the culture and beliefs of Islam, hoping to build on commonalities between religions. She visited several communities which had never seen or even heard of a Muslim.

"In one town where I was invited to address a Sunday church service, a huge uproar broke out over whether I should be allowed to speak. In the end, I did, and after the service, when I was greeting people on the way out, several had tears in their eyes and they said "We didn't realize you are just like us!"

From the reaction to her presentations at endless conferences and meetings around Manitoba, it seemed that the policy of outreach was paying off.

Shahina Siddiqui notes with pride that there are now two Mosques in the city, and prayers at two Winnipeg Universities and the Health Sciences Centre. She also wrote numerous pamphlets about Islam (among them a guide for Journalists covering Islam) and helped to bring about the creation of a Muslim Outreach and Education program.

In 1995, she instituted the first week long training session in social work and counselling for Imams and Muslim social service providers.

A highlight of her work was the first educational retreat for Muslim youth, which brought forty outstanding young people from around the world to Winnipeg for a month of study in the summer of 1997. Thirteen Muslim scholars comprised their teachers. She also helped establish the first Islamic private school in Manitoba in 1996–Alhijra Islamic school which now has 200 students from kindergarten to grade nine.

And then, September 11, 2001.

"On that day, I...we ...truly became "The Other."

It has been an astonishing experience.

"Many Muslims were killed in the attacks by terrorists on the twin towers in New York, but we alone never had the chance to grieve, never felt the comfort of public understanding for our losses.

Muslims everywhere were thrust into guilt by association, into an awesome backlash which was verbal, physical, both subtle and brutally direct. Suddenly, children were harassed at school, and there was name calling in streets and offices. Suddenly, if you were Muslim in appearance, you would find security following you around the mall. Young women wearing the hijab were afraid to wait at bus stops.

Very few Canadians had real relationships with, so the disinformation that followed 911 was easy for many people to accept. Whatever bigotry and racism lurked beneath the surface saw an opportunity for expression. The labelling was especially hurtful. The words "Islamic" and "terrorist" became attached to each other in the media, and the idea of Islam seemed suddenly no more than a battle cry, a collection of mindless creatures in need of taming.

Some Canadians found Shahina Siddiqui's writings about Islam after 911 offensive. There were late night phone calls, ugly letters with graphic death threats.

Like many other Muslims, she discovered she was being watched by the Canadian Security and Intelligence Service.

Though freedom of speech became much more difficult to practise, believing that neither silence nor denial would assuage the crisis for Muslims, she continued to speak and write about tolerance, publishing in the *Winnipeg Free Press*, the *National Post* , the *Calgary Herald*, *Canadian Dimension* and many American Muslim newspapers and magazines.

"I fell back on the tradition of the Prophet here. He taught us how to communicate in traumatic circumstances: be polite in your argument; remember that knowledge overtakes darkness, and do not stoop to the level of someone who considers himself your enemy."

She has remained unafraid to say what her instincts tell her is necessary.

When she was asked on a CBC open line show where she found the hope to go on, she answered there was hope in "tuning out the media and tuning into God's love and presence in our lives."

After the bombings in London which killed 56 people in July of 2005, she wrote in the Winnipeg Free Press that

"The most severe threat to Muslims is from Muslims who manipulate the young minds and manipulate the teachings of our peaceful religion to carry out criminal acts leaving all of us to face the consequences. We must isolate and confront extremists at both ends of the spectrum."

For her work after 911 in fostering understanding between Muslims and other religious and cultural groups in Winnipeg, Shahina Siddiqui was awarded the highly respected YMCA-YWCA Peace Medal in 2002. She considers her biggest challenge now the direct threat to the civil rights of Muslims and all Canadians that has developed as a result of post 911 pre-occupation with "national security."

"One day, while travelling by plane, it was time to say one of the obligatory daily prayers, and I found myself questioning whether I should do it. It was then I realized that I was afraid for the well being of my family, and it dawned on me what the mental state must be of anyone who has been handicapped by language or the experience of ethnic cleansing, war or persecution."

She remains concerned not just for the five young Muslim men who have been held in Canadian jails without charges or trials, but for the loss of due process of law which she feels puts all citizens of Canada at risk.

"I hope and pray that Canada will return to being the country I thought it was. I am looking forward to the time when my children and grandchildren will not have to think of themselves as "the other."

This country is my home, and if I need to work harder to bring this about, I will do it."

"Peace is an ongoing process, and for me it's not a matter of choice, it's a duty. I take it one step at a time, focusing on small goals as part of a wider vision.

"I'm so blessed to have a supportive family; my husband and son who never tire of taking me places and picking me up, my daughter in law, who is a great joy to me. Sometimes I get weary, or I feel intimidated by fresh problems.

But I'll never stop, because working for peace brings me peace."

Paul Soubry

. . . .

It is October 22, 2003 and a perfect, golden day for the University of Manitoba's fall convocation.

It's also one of the most splendid days in Paul Soubry's life.

Today, surrounded by his family, he will be dressed in an elegant red and white academic gown with a black tasselled cap to replace the simple black robe he has always worn on formal university occasions.

While he's taken a lot of courses at different universities, after today he will be fully recognized as a formerly educated man, a Doctor of Laws, having received an honorary degree from a Canadian university which is grateful for his many services.

"Receiving this degree is something I never thought would happen. I always regretted not having one and felt awkward sitting on the platform as chairman at convocations with just a plain black robe, without a multi-coloured hood.

Today I got the works. How wonderful!"

Paul Soubry, LLD, was never that interested in school as a youngster When he'd had as much schooling as he could take as a lad in his native Belgium, restless and yearning for adventure, he just "moved on."

And on. And on, as far as Canada, where he would distinguish himself as an icon of management, a master of the export business, a one man economic engine, and the very spirit of volunteerism and community service For which in 2002, he received the Queens Golden Jubilee Medal.

At his special convocation in 2003, Dr. Soubry confided in his address to the students who were graduating with him that he was one of the most fortunate persons on earth.

"Perfect strangers had enough trust and confidence in me, that they were willing to give an immigrant, without a formal post secondary education, a chance and were willing to invest in his training.

While I worked hard and was totally dedicated to my job, I owe everything to the many people along the way, my mentors."

He told the graduates that they too were indebted to others who had made their education possible, and he implored them to accept their moral obligation, to find a way to give something back to their community.

They could tell he really meant it.

That's because he was preaching what he had practised all his life.

His thirst for adventure brought him to Canada, but his Uncle Emile also helped.

Emile Soubry had immigrated to Canada in the twenties, eventually owning a grain and feed business and settling in a bustling. St.Boniface across the river from Winnipeg.

In 1948, young Paul decided he would visit Uncle Emile, learn as much as he could about the grain business, and eventually return to Belgium to "make something of himself."

He didn't realize then that a unique education in "real life" had already begun to prepare him for future success as an international business man.

Few children have ever had to share their homes with soldiers of opposing occupying armies, but Paul Soubry did.

He was 10 years old, attending Flemish school and living with his aunts in Bruges when the German army invaded Belgium. In May of that year, his parents hurriedly collected their children and fled to the Spanish border of France. By September, they realized they would have to return and wait things out.

"When we arrived home, our house was occupied by German soldiers. There was no choice. We had to share it with them." he recalls.

When Belgium was liberated in 1945, the roommates changed. This time the Soubry family shared their home with the men of the liberating American Army. He couldn't know it then, but the adaptability required by those contrasting experiences would come in very handy in international business. So did the training he got from the Boy Scouts, which provided him with steady guidance and the value of simple virtues.

Paul was a King's Scout, an achievement that gives him pleasure to this day.

"As a boy, I found Scouts much more instructive and fun than the schoolroom. It was incredibly important because the scout masters impressed on us the value of being a leader, the need to solve your own problems independently but still work as a team..

"I can still remember living out in the bush for two days at a time, facing a Scout leader who expected me to observe and remember all kinds of details, like the number of cows in a certain field. It was excellent discipline.

Some of these lessons I've called on all my life."

In Belgium, birth order was very important.

"My father was the youngest of eight children, which is

very different from being the oldest. It is much less important. I, on the other hand, was the oldest child of six in my family, and I had to prove I could do something significant.

When young Paul applied for a visa for the visit with Uncle Emile in Canada, he got back an immigrant's visa, a bonus of which he wasn't really aware.

The first trip to St Boniface was no holiday. Emile handed him a shovel and put him to work unloading grain cars, and, worried that Paul had no English, enrolled him in a local business college. Working and studying left time for four or five hours sleep a night.

Paul Soubry also found himself swept up in the Manitoba's historic flood of 1950, an experience that illustrated the rewards of "pulling together in tough times." All he remembers now is being called to direct emergency traffic, which he did wearing his Boy Scout uniform.

In the fall of 1950, he returned briefly to visit his family in Belgium.

Paul knew that his father had hoped that he would stay home and work with him, but after short visit there, he wanted to return to Canada, where a job was already waiting for him.

He could speak both official languages fluently by now, and he felt he wouldn't be considered a foreigner. He also fit in with the spirit of volunteerism he'd found among Canadians.

"It must have been very painful for my father to let me go, but he never discussed it with me.

"I sensed that, although I'd been born and had grown up somewhere else, success was more possible in Canada. In Belgium things were much more rigid; the class system was very hard to navigate. There were too many barriers to accomplishment, and looking back, I know I could never have done there what I have done here.

With no degrees and no connections, I was not going to be anyone's CEO.

"At one point, I decided I would not only adapt to Canadian customs, I would become more Canadian than Canadian."

The first job he had secured in Canada was with a well known agricultural company called Cockshutt Plow Ltd. whose managers saw the usefulness of his European background and hired him as an export trainee in their Brantford, Ontario operations.

"I was 22 years old and boarding with a family there. Of course I was single and I was all drive, and I remember telling them I'd be president of the company by the time I was 45. They told me I was crazy. I guess they were right. It took me till I was 46!"

It was at Cockshutt that Paul met the man who taught him the meaning of mentorship and provided him with the basic blueprint for success in business

"The bosses made me a go-fer for the Vice President of Sales, a man named Jim Hill. I can't even measure what I owe him. He taught me on the job everything about how to run a business, how to deal with people, how to be patient and dedicated to the company. He was unbelievably generous to me. He was an exceptional man!"

Jim Hill offered a model of management Paul Soubry never forgot.

It was also at Cockshutt Plow that he learned to "keep his eye on the job right above him" so as to be ready when it became available.

After a stint in the Calgary branch, he was transferred to Montreal, and later assigned a territory manager's position in Sherbrooke, Quebec.

An illness landed him in the Sherbrooke General Hospital which, the young bachelor couldn't help but notice, was full of pretty nurses.

"There was one in particular who caught my eye. I thought of her as 'The Face.'"

I was in isolation. It seemed to be her job to come to the

door, peek in and see I was getting the right care. So every-day I'd just see The Face looking at me from the doorway. It was a beautiful face."

The face belonged to nurse Louise Fortier, who would soon be avidly pursued by the recovered former patient.

Their courtship reflected some of the many difficulties of inter-cultural marriage.

"In Quebec we had a saying, 'Qui prend mari, prend pays' which translates as "who takes a husband, takes a country." Louise offers.

"I was very close to my family, and he was so far away from his. My life was in Montreal, and he travelled around the world. Yes, he spoke French, but in some ways he seemed more British than French. It was the formal Belgian in him. And anyone could see he was a confirmed workaholic. He never talked about his work as though it was a job.

But he was so jovial, so happy, so well mannered.

I finally said yes, even though I was wondering where this would take me."

They were married December 21, 1957.

Louise need not have worried about Paul's attitude toward family ties. After the wedding, her new husband blew his entire performance bonus on a honeymoon in Belgium so his bride could meet her newly acquired family.

It would turn out that he wrote his parents every week, never forgot a birthday, and, even in those days when an appointment was necessary to call Overseas, he telephoned the family on special occasions.

The marriage would produce six healthy, well adjusted and successful children: Mark, Gregory, Ann, Paul, Marina, and Veronique.

When Cockshutt Plow was acquired in 1962 by the White Motor Corporation, Paul Soubry survived the acquisition, a skill for which he would later become legendary. He continued with White as export Manager, and eventually moved through the position of Vice President, Marketing to the appointment as President in 1976.

He learned along the way that there were adjustments to be made in business as well as social life. He would have to adapt to major cultural differences from business to business.

"Europeans could have a business meeting in the blink of an eye, spontaneously, anytime, anywhere. You could meet at 9 or 2. Who cared? All you needed were the people involved. In Canada, like the US, you needed a table and chairs, a room and a formal appointment."

I made it a point to "Adapt! Adapt!" and of course I learned to pay careful attention to internal politics."

In 1977, Paul Soubry was recruited as President and CEO of Versatile Farm Equipment in Winnipeg, a company well known for its production of large machines such as tractors, combines, and swathers. Under his leadership, Versatile further expanded its operations into the USA and Australia and exported their Canadian products overseas.

"We were certainly one of Manitoba's major exporters; we were given the Manitoba Export Award and twice received the prestigious Canada Export Award. Shipments increased over time to thirty countries with an annual value of $300 million dollars.

"There were around 1200 employees on the payroll at Versatile when I was there. I made it a point to learn as many names as I could. I tried to walk through the plant everyday and always said hello and listened to what people had to say to me. It seems like a small thing, but it can make a big positive difference in the working environment."

In 1987, the agricultural operations of Versatile were acquired by the Ford Motor Company. Once again he survived, and two years later was appointed Chairman of the Board and President of Ford New Holland Canada Ltd.

The next few years brought still more mergers with international companies. When New Holland Canada Ltd was established, he was named Vice President and General Manager during that period, Versatile again expanded its product line, adding two wheel drive tractors which were transferred from Ford's Antwerp, Belgium plant to Winnipeg as well as industrial loader/backhoe tractors from Romeo, Michigan.

By December of 1995, at the age of 65, Paul Soubry felt he had contributed as much to marketing, management and corporate life as he could, and retired.

"The corporate world had offered just the right mix of security and risk for me. And I loved the teamwork that's so necessary in a business environment.

"Of course, the kind of career I had is not an easy one. In some ways, all your work is like a walk in the sand; you can look back, and your footprints may seem to have disappeared.

And since you are always providing a service, as many a good man can tell you, they can always say "thank you very much" and you can find yourself swallowed up by the system.

It's a risk, but a risk I enjoyed. I was very, very lucky."

Along the way Paul Soubry had shared his expertise and enthusiasm with countless local, provincial and national organizations, most of them promoting Canada, its domestic manufacturing and its exports. Chairing the Canadian Exporters Association was a personal highlight for him because It was "kind of a patriotic thing to do."

The other was the CRB, (Canadian Industrial Renewal Board) where he became vice chairman.

He also enjoyed his work with governmental task forces which called on his travel, his contacts, and his experience in promoting international trade.

Among other organizations, he offered executive direction to the CFIEI, the Canadian Farm Industrial Equipment Institute, and PIMA (Prairie Implement Manufacturers' Association) where he could encourage all the agricultural manufacturers in Canada to develop the data, statistics and products appropriate to world markets.

His volunteer activities were many and diverse. Besides chairing a multitude of exporting associations, he served on the Board of Winnipeg's Victoria Hospital and on the advisory board to the Government of Manitoba's Industrial Technology Center, where he could focus on improving the national and international business management practises of Manitoba companies and at the same time work with ideas and new opportunities.

In 1996, the lifelong workaholic formed his own small enterprise, the Soubry management consulting company, concentrating on SME's (Small and Medium Enterprises)

But another opportunity soon appeared which he found much more attractive than working for himself.

He still remembers the phone call from Manitoba's then Minister of Education, Linda Macintosh wondering whether Paul Soubry would consider bringing some of his proven business expertise to a place on the University of Manitoba's Board of Governors. It would just mean a few meetings a year, the Minister said.

"Right," says Louise, laughing. "In fact, the University of Manitoba became his next child!"

He was appointed to the Board of Governors by Order in Council in March of 1996 and became its chair in 97, serving in that capacity for the next five years. He had absolutely no academic background or experience, but he was a quick study, and an old hand at motivating committees, shaking hands with VIPS, and, of course, marketing.

In a short time, Paul Soubry was confident he could bring a different approach to the University of Manitoba's affairs, supporting the President and her administration. And no one was surprised when he did just that.

The timing was right; it was the era of deficit slashing. Money was tight; current grants were not enough to sustain programs there was a need for just the kind of innovation and long term planning Paul Soubry could encourage.

In the years he would serve on the Board of Governors,

however, The University managed to surprise Paul Soubry.

In the corporate world, the bottom line was the important thing, But in this new world, the major responsibility was the formation of people.

"It was a pleasure and so stimulating, to see how the institution operated, and I came to appreciate the great people keep it going. Coming straight from industry after retirement, I learned a lot about a different environment. Business has not really discovered equivalents to tenure, academic freedom, sabbaticals and administrative leaves, but I have learned these things seem to work.'

In his view, the University has an ongoing need for marketing strategies so that politicians and the community at large appreciate its true value as a centre of excellence and as an economic engine.

"When my service to the Board of Governors was over, I was truly reluctant to say goodbye. To this day, when I'm driving on Pembina Highway, my car still wants to turn on Chancellor Matheson Drive."

"Overall, Canada has been a land of unlimited opportunity for me and for many others" Paul Soubry muses.

"Canada has been my home for fifty seven years. How lucky can one man get?"

Dr. Emöke J.E. Szathmáry

· ·

There are many ways to describe a large moment in life.

Call it what you will; breakthrough, epiphany, a revelation. Emöke Szathmáry, 10th President and Vice Chancellor of the University of Manitoba, had such a moment at the age of nineteen.

It brought a blazing clarity to the future direction of her personal and professional life.

To understand her excitement, it's first necessary to know that, just as she was gathering momentum as a newly minted anthropology student, somebody told her that her profession was dead.

Quite naturally, she objected.

True, her parents and their friends were wondering what on earth a young woman could do with a degree in Anthropology. True, as she puts it now, "There were certainly no ads in the *Globe and Mail* or the *Welland Tribune* for anyone with that qualification."

"But I did not believe I was embracing a moribund profession; I thought my elders were wrong."

This was a handy lesson for a woman who would eventually become the President of a University, where differences of opinion between generations can be plentiful and heated.

Emöke Szathmáry shared her "signal moment" with her colleagues in an essay she wrote for the American Journal of Physical Anthropology at the beginning of the 21st century.

She took her readers back to her undergraduate classroom at the University of Toronto:

"My professor had already completed the biological portion of the course and was telling us about the views of Emile Durkheim, who claimed that human beings have a number of intrinsic needs, but different societies have developed different ways to provide for those needs.

Biological and social perspectives came together for me that moment, because if human beings are all members of the same species, they all have the same intrinsic survival needs– which different societies meet differently-this deduction had to mean that cultural differences cannot make one group of human beings biologically inferior to another, whatever advantages one culture has attained compared to another!

The die was cast: the next year I was registered in the Honours Anthropology program….by the end of my fourth year, I knew I wanted to study human population genetics at the graduate level and I decided to do it within the framework of Anthropology."

"It was a cosmic discovery for me, a lightning bolt, and only a 19 year old could be so certain that this insight had the answers to everything." she remembers now.

She may have been just nineteen, but Emöke Szathmáry was entitled to take the idea that human beings were intrinsically equal very personally. She could relate easily to people whose value was discounted.

It had happened to her as far back as she could remember

in Canada.

Not only was she a tall, olive skinned and dark eyed child who could pass for an "Indian" (which she was not) in a land of blue eyed blondes, but the economic status of her family as immigrants had shaped a childhood and adolescence experienced "on the wrong side of the tracks."

And she had learned from her experiences that "what was in my mind, my ability to think and to know was the only thing that could not be taken from me."

The University of Manitoba would eventually hold out a powerful attraction for someone with exactly that experience and those values. There was a strong intellectual appeal as well.

When the university was searching for a new president in 1996, it could boast some excellent work in human genetics, including early work in serology and cytology. She had first heard about the University of Manitoba in a fourth year human genetics class, when the professor told them of the discovery of a method by U of M scientists to prevent Rh disease in newborns. Further, she knew the U of M outstanding in life sciences generally.

Emöke Szathmáry had been offered a job in the University of Manitoba's Anthropology department much earlier, in 1972, and she had travelled to Winnipeg then and left with a favourable impression.

"Every University in Canada or elsewhere reflects the character of its city. From its founding, the city that grew around the confluence of the Assiniboine and Red Rivers has been marked by a diversity of people and a diversity of their dwelling places. It's remarkable that few understand that diversity marks Winnipeg still," she says.

Even then, Emöke Szathmáry was a huge fan of diversity.

"But I wanted to finish my thesis then more than I wanted to teach full time."

She and her husband decided to stay in Ontario.

The university to which she returned as President in 1996

was a much different, more complex place than it had been in the seventies.

"I arrived nine months after a devastating strike that had lasted for six weeks. The University of Manitoba had lost a lot of community support. Labour issues tend to polarize this city quickly – just remember the strike of 1919. Remember this was the first English speaking university where professors unionized, and I had never worked in a campus where the faculty were union members.

I knew the huge dimensions of the task. The University had to rebuild to be appreciated, refocus its energies on teaching and research, and build bridges between many important interest groups.

But of course an anthropologist is first an observer; you can imagine what a challenge it presented!"

Emöke Szathmáry was comparatively undaunted by the University's crisis not only because she approached life with the discipline of an anthropologist; she had also faced more than her share of extreme challenges before she had even set foot in elementary school.

* * * * * * * *

Three unlikely factors first brought the Szathmáry family to Canada from Hungary; a world war, a revolution in South America, and a history of Tuberculosis.

"My mother and I left Hungary in November of 1944 when I was 10 months old and as the Russians were moving in from the East. People like us were known then as displaced persons or "DPs"–it was not a flattering term–and we lived in a "DP" camp in the British sector of Germany for a long time–from 1946 until 1951.

"My parents, both of whom held university degrees had been accepted into Bolivia and were offered jobs at a university there, but a revolution broke out in La Paz, which put an abrupt end to that possibility.

"It's fair to say that many of those who lost everything in the war hoped to go to the United States, but that wasn't possible either. If there had been TB in your family, the US would accept you, but only if you agreed to leave the ill person behind.

Canada was the first country to accept families with a history of TB. My brother had had it. My mother was adamant that no child would be left behind. We could all come here together. So we did.

Her parents were convinced that Canada was a land of milk and honey. The country had, after all, expressed an official interest in welcoming professionals, and they were both qualified Physical Education teachers.

"A farmer in Ontario had volunteered to sponsor their travel if they would help with the spring planting, but as events turned out, they arrived in Halifax harbour having missed the planting season, and he lost interest in transporting them to their original destination. In order to get there, they accepted jobs picking tobacco. So our first home in this country was a Tobacco kiln!

There were few supports in place for immigrants then and life was more or less a gamble. I was seven and a half years old, looking after three younger siblings. My father and brothers were Unitarians, and my mother and my sister were Catholic, but when my mother fell ill and was hospitalized, it was the local Baptists who rode to the rescue. I'll never forget them."

Emöke Szathmáry remembers quite a bit about the life in the refugee camps but a great deal about growing up as a "new Canadian" in Ontario.

She remembers what it was like to speak no English, which she mastered by the fifth grade, and what it was like to take her classes in a one room school house, and later attend five schools in two years.

Money was in very short supply, but family bonds were close.

"One thing we could afford to do was go camping, which suited my dad, because he loved to tell us campfire stories. He wanted us to remember Hungary, where we came from and what made us different. My mother was the great narrator of Hungarian history – while we did dishes together.

"I was fascinated to learn that seven Hungarian tribes had moved from Asia to what is now Hungary, that the Hungarians had raided all over Europe until they were defeated in France, that they had had shamanistic religion before 1000 AD.

"Both my parents were very strong individuals, though in different ways. Thanks to them, I knew my background; I knew difference was good, and I refused to be defined by what other people thought or wanted.

For example even in the peer pressure of adolescence, I absolutely refused to give up my name.

Because of my mother, who was an educated and lively woman, I never felt disadvantaged by gender. Maybe it helped that in Hungarian, as in Uralic languages, there are no he/she pronouns; on paper, the contexct tells whether one is male or female. And my parents expected achievement regardless of the sex of their children."

The family took good advantage of inexpensive activities available to everyone in the community. The house was always full of library books. Emöke discovered sports, especially basketball at which she excelled, and the challenges of Girl Guides, where she eventually earned the coveted status of the Gold Cord.

Emöke and her family became citizens on November 12, 1956.

"That was a time when it seemed particularly fortunate to be here.

The Communists had moved into Hungary in 1945 and took power in 1947. The Hungarian revolution of 1956 really tested Canada's capacity for refugees; this country was very, very good to Hungarians."

But the changes that immigration forced on the Szathmáry family took their toll. Emöke's parents divorced when she was 13.

"It was hard to accept, but I think it also intensified my interest in who I was and where I came from."

During her student years, she happened to hear a broadcast on CBC radio which gave her a chance to think even more carefully about her identity.

It was a serialization of John Marlyn's book Under the Ribs of Death a novel set in the North End of Winnipeg in the period leading up to the stock market crash of 1929. First published in 1959, and re-released in 1993, it detailed the wretched experiences of one Sandor Hunyadi also a Hungarian refugee, living in what amounted to a ghetto of foreigners.

"I could relate to him in many ways. He was a young man who was trying to learn how to be Canadian; he was teased and beaten up for being different, as my brothers were, and as I would have been, if I had hadn't been so tall. I knew also how he felt when he caught a glimpse of the other end of town and its vast green lawns.

But we reached different conclusions about what it meant to become Canadian. Sandor thought it meant abandoning everything he had been before –he changed his name to Alex Hunter – and he scorned his father's values, which were rooted in the writings of the world's great thinkers.

I believed you could be Canadian without doing any of those things."

With the help of a scholarship Emöke enrolled in the University of Toronto, distinguished herself for academic achievement and graduated with a Bachelor of Arts, Honours Anthropology in 1968.

"That graduation had one unforgettable moment when one of the graduating student leaders ripped up his diploma on stage because, he said, it was useless and he felt nothing but contempt for it.

"As one who had enjoyed the satisfaction of learning very early, and one who knew better than to take anything for granted, of course I felt differently"

She would return to the University of Toronto to earn a Ph.D. (Anthropology) and still a third time in 2001 to receive an Honorary Doctor of Laws for her achievements and contributions to her profession. In 2004, her undergraduate college, St. Michael's, conferred on her an honorary Doctor of Sacred Letters.

These honours and others she would receive celebrated work in biological anthropology, work which could fairly be described as well ahead of its time.

"What thrilled me was not the recognition itself, but the fact that my research had actually caused people to ask fresh questions about important things, that I was able to interest others in the questions that interested me, such as "Who were the original colonizers of North America?" and "How does culture channel the transmission of genes?"

Humans had not evolved in then Americas; they came here from elsewhere and previous scholars had relied on evidence derived from bones or teeth, but my concentration was on genetic evidence.

Among other things, it showed that the indigenous people of the Americas can claim that their genetic profiles have been shaped by events on the North and South American continents. They have some genes that occur nowhere else in the world. They were not just another wave of immigrants, as some have claimed, any more than the first humans who moved into Europe from the Middle East can be dismissed as just another wave of immigrants.

The ancestors of the First Nations and the Inuit came here before anyone else was here and they took dominion over this continent."

Emöke Szathmáry was also ahead of her time in her intense and early interest in the etiology of diabetes among Aboriginal people.

"Nobody in Canada was really concerned about this as a health issue, but I knew because of my understanding of genetics and complex diseases that since it was an issue in the US, it would become. A problem here."

At the convocation which invested her with the honorary Doctor of Laws degree, she recalled the prolonged post war poverty of her family and entreated her fellow graduates to remember that war could dispossess anyone, rob them of work or means.

"If you come across people from reduced socio-economic circumstances," she said, "Never discount them. They are just like you and me."

It was the lesson of her own life, and the lesson she had learned again from the Aboriginal people among whom she did extensive research, especially the Ottawa, the Ojibwa and Dogrib peoples in Northern Ontario and in the Northwest Territories.

In 1978-79, Emöke Szathmáry had done field work among the Dogrib people in NWT, had enjoyed their generous co-operation in her research and had also made friends with some of her interpreters.

"My work took me back there in 1985, just one week after the death of my father. It was a painful time because we had never resolved our differences. I happened to notice, that when I went off for a long walk at the end of the day, or sat on a hillside musing, somebody joined me. Whoever was with me didn't speak; they were just "there."

It is our custom to grieve alone, by ourselves, but, as I would learn later, it was their custom to keep company with someone mourning a loss.

I was never left alone. It still moves me to remember this."

What she learned about the causes of Type 2 Diabetes among aboriginal peoples provided material for dozens of articles and her research on this and other topics led to three books co-authored with colleagues.

From the Anishinabe and Dene peoples, she also acquired an immense appreciation for aboriginal cultures and indigenous wisdom.

As she moved through graduate school and teaching appointments throughout the seventies and eighties, she discovered retroactively the importance of the unconscious feminism she had learned from her mother.

"I wouldn't say I suffered active discrimination because I was a woman, but there was a certain bittersweet quality about being judged by a man's standards. For example, during the first year I taught at McMaster University, I had a baby, I looked after my nine year old and my husband as would any working wife, I published a demanding paper, and I developed two new courses in Anthropology. There was no maternity leave available then; that's just the way it was.

"The annual performance review mattered, because the University's merit assessment influenced salary. Judged by a man's standards, I was rated average that year."

But time was also kind. Later, when women were being belatedly moved into positions of authority, I was ready to accept that challenge."

Appointments at Trent University, at McMaster, (where she was named Chair of the department of Anthropology in 1985) and terms as Dean of Social Science at The University of Western Ontario, and as Provost and Vice President (Academic) again at McMaster, combined with expertise in Aboriginal issues may have helped to bring Emöke Szathmáry to the attention of Manitoba's Presidential search committee in 1995.

"There were a number of candidates who met the dozen or more requirements and could have done the job; I guess I was the best fit. In 1996, they made me "the offer I couldn't refuse." she smiles.

The responsibilities of repairing the damages done by the strike shortly before her appointment were an immediate challenge to her leadership. And then came the Flood of

1997.

"It was a highly instructive crisis. It reinforced the vastness of the risks run by institutions like this, and the need for really thorough preparations. We weren't worried only about buildings; there were all those valuable research animals on the University's experimental farm at Glenlea that needed to be evacuated. The trouble was that the flood unfolded in the birth season, and many animals couldn't be moved. We had to build up the dike by at least a metre, maintain earth moving machines around the clock and we had to be ready to get those animals on barges within half an hour if the need arose."

It was tense, but the Flood of '97 passed, clearing the way for other pressing problems on the president's desk.

"I can't take credit for all of it, because so many other people have been involved but the University has managed to advance on quite a few fronts since then.

"I organized the President's Task Force on strategic planning and its subsequent Report which clarified some of the major challenges which followed the era of deficit slashing and ever shrinking budgets.

"The public hearings we held were amazingly well attended; 160 private citizens presented at those hearings, a clear indication that people were really interested in the university's future.

"I recognised that organizations in Winnipeg, including the University, suffered from "perimeter-itis" a kind of benign neglect of interested parties outside the city itself. I decided to visit alumni in the rural areas, including Brandon, Thompson, Steinbach and Portage la Prairie.

"It dawned on me that we had 100,000 living graduates and that only 10% of them were members of the Alumni Association. Now everyone's a member.

"It's impossible, really, to cite any one recent step forward as more important than others, but the success of the Capital Campaign ($ 237 million dollars) was hugely encouraging, as is the progress we've made around Smartpark. That high tech research park was proposed by our Board way back in 1982 but it only came into being in 1999. By 2006, it's expected that about 800 people will be working there."

Keeping abreast of academic and intellectual issues across the country doesn't leave much time for play, but Emöke Szathmáry enjoys reading the currently popular novels by Kathy Reich and Patricia Cornwell which feature female anthropologists and coroners as their detectives.

She also takes time to keep an eye on developments in human population genetics.

"To this day, I remain a knowledge junkie."

She remains faithful also to her convictions about the value of diversity and the need to respect identity.

She remembers an encounter with an elderly gentleman, a retiree of the U of M, who approached her at a reception shortly after her appointment as President in July of 1996. He spoke to her in Hungarian.

"He had known my father. He'd been a soldier and he had been in prison after the war. He wanted to tell me that Canada, specifically the city of Winnipeg, was the first place where people had treated him like a man, like a real human being."

I think he was curious to see if I was the kind of person who would behave in the same way.

I think that's as much as we can hope to do."